Derbyshire Customs

90p

By the same author:
DERBYSHIRE TRADITIONS
GHOSTS OF DERBYSHIRE
HAUNTED DERBYSHIRE

Other Dalesman books of related interest:
LANCASHIRE LEGENDS
LEGENDS OF DERBYSHIRE
LEGENDS OF NOTTINGHAMSHIRE
LEGENDS OF THE LAKE COUNTIES
YORKSHIRE CUSTOMS
YORKSHIRE LEGENDS

Derbyshire Customs

by

Clarence Daniel

Dalesman Books
1976

The Dalesman Publishing Company Ltd.,
Clapham (via Lancaster), North Yorkshire.
First published 1976

ISBN: 0 85206 358 X

Printed in Great Britain by Galava Printing Company Limited,
Hallam Road, Nelson, Lancashire.

Contents

The cover picture of Morris dancers at Bakewell is by E. Hector Kyme. The back cover photograph is of well-dressing at Wormhill (copyright, Davy and United Engineering Co. Ltd.).

Photographs in the text are on pages 33-36 and 53-56.

Introduction

FOLK-LORE is a fascinating field of research into human psychology. While it seldom concerns itself with the famous names and notable events of history, it sometimes represents them in caricature. Many of our nursery rhymes were literary lampoons aimed at ridiculing prominent personalities who had offended against public taste. "Mary, Mary, quite contrary" portrayed the efforts of Queen Mary to reintroduce the pre-Reformation faith. Others were sinister satires on current happenings. "Ring a ring o' roses" depicted the horrors of the Great Plague.

But, basically, folk-lore treats upon the simple faith and innocent fancies of ordinary people. Not only does the student seek to diagnose their superstitions, but he attempts to preserve a picture of their pastimes and the family festivals which occupied periods of limited leisure to give them a brief respite from the pressures of poverty, insecurity, social repression and domestic drudgery.

Folk-lore can sometimes supplement the study of history, even though its traditions are suspect by reason of the fact that they rest upon oral rather than written testimony. So often we find that a story which has been told and re-told becomes exaggerated and distorted. Important facts are omitted and worthless fictions added, due to faulty memories, so that each repetition reduces its reliability and the kernel of truth it contains is difficult to discover because of the shell of faulty evidence which has grown around it.

The same principle applies to customs. They have been altered, adapted, or re-shaped during the passage of years, and with each change the original meaning has become a little more obscure. They began with holy days and often ended as holidays. Some had their birth in family grief as attested by the funeral garland; some expressed the instinct of propitiation as in the case of well-dressings or perambulations; others perpetuated some national event as illustrated by the Garland ceremony at Castleton; while some were intended to underline parish anniversaries of religious or civil significance.

Some of the customs described in the following pages are still observed: others have become obsolete. Those which have survived are almost as much a part of the Derbyshire scene as the limestone dales and millstone-grit escarpments of the Peak District, or the smoother contours of the southern landscapes. They have become part and pattern of its ever changing social life— a gift bequeathed from earlier generations who found pride in preserving something of the past for the enjoyment of those living in the present.

1.

Derbyshire Customs through the Year

SOME of the customs and annual happenings in Derbyshire are decided by certain saints' days and vary slightly from year to year, while others take place on fixed dates. The Peak Park Planning Board, Aldern House, Bakewell, publishes a useful free leaflet of events each year and this supplies the exact dates. Those wishing to acquaint themselves of all or any particular occasion, are recommended to apply for this literature, enclosing a s/a envelope for the favour of a reply. The leaflet also supplies information on village markets and museums, exhibitions and carnivals, stately homes and sheep dog trials, fairs, fetes and folk-dancing.

The annual pageant of events begins on Ascension Day at Tissington with a springtime well-dressing and this was the village responsible for inaugurating the custom as we know it today. Tradition asserts that the custom was revived during the 17th century as an act of gratitude for the fact that either the springs never failed during a time of drought, or the village escaped infection during an epidemic of plague. Both these circumstances we find are attested in general terms in contemporary parochial records. During the mid-eighteenth century the custom consisted of hoops of wood decorated with artificial flowers and rosettes, and sometimes containing a rustic rhyme extolling the virtues and value of water, being suspended over the wells. The custom was experimental and exploratory and developed into the more sophisticated techniques which have provided the model for other villages that subsequently adopted the idea.

The next village to claim our attention is Castleton with its Garland Ceremony held on Oak Apple Day (May 29th). This is another springtime festival and is known to have been observed in neighbouring villages and in many other parts of the country. I remember when schoolchildren in Eyam wore sprigs of oak in their lapels or sprays pinned to their dresses, to guarantee not being stung by older children armed with bunches of nettles. Now the Garland Ceremony, with its central figure encased in a grotesque armour of oak leaves and flowers, is exclusive to this picturesque village with its castle and caves and vague memories of visiting royalty and knights tilting at a great tournament. Therefore it would be difficult to find a more fitting environment for this strange ceremony from the past.

Students of folk-lore argue as to whether it is a relic of Druid ritual, recalling the fact that they worshipped in groves of oak; a pagan ceremony to propitiate their gods of growth and fertility; or whether it is a survival of a charade acted in many villages to commemorate the Restoration of King Charles. Whatever the reason, it is an occasion well worth a visit.

As the summer progresses, we move on to Wirksworth for Spring Bank Holiday. This town was formerly the centre of the lead-mining industry for the Low Peak and still preserves the Moot Hall where Barmote Courts are held and the brass dish which was the standard measure for lead-ore. Wirksworth was also the home of Samuel and Elizabeth Evans who figure prominently in the pages of "Adam Bede" written by their niece, Mary Ann Evans, or "George Eliot". Well-dressing has a long history in this township and its early screens may have been assessed by Samuel and his wife. The custom was initiated in 1827 as an expression of appreciation of the generosity of several benefactors who defrayed the cost of a water scheme in which the supply was conveyed through wooden pipes to stand taps in the village, causing the custom to become known as "tap-dressing".

Susan Marsden, evidently a devotee of well-dressing, left £100, the interest of which was to be annually disbursed in prizes to encourage juvenile efforts, thus ensuring that the custom would have apprentices who would grow up to be masters of the craft.

Simultaneously with Wirksworth, well-dressings are held at Monyash which was once the centre of lead-mining for the High Peak. Barmote Courts were held here for the management of the mines by men who had developed their own system of industrial democracy. Monyash was once the home of John Gratton, a 17th century Quaker, who suffered much abuse and frequent imprisonment for his faith, and a small Quaker Chapel (now disused) was serving as the venue for an excellent exhibition of village treasures one Spring Bank Holiday. It was a feature of the annual Village Market organised for charity. Which brings me to the point that well-dressing was introduced in recent years as a part of this activity.

As its name implies, Ashford-in-the Water is an ideal location for a survival of water worship, for the village is as picturesque as its name with the River Wye weaving its way through wood and meadow and slipping quietly beneath its several bridges. After an unsuccessful attempt in 1930 to revive the custom of well-dressing, it became securely established in the 1950s. Students from the nearby Thornbridge Hall Teachers' Training College helped in the early days and produced some highly commendable results. Sometimes the floral artists have departed from tradition, using unorthodox material and unconventional styles of presentation, transgressing the strict rule that no manufactured articles should be used in the composition of the pictures. Nevertheless, they have attained a high standard of efficiency.

The wells are blessed on Trinity Sunday and visitors should not miss seeing the ancient funeral garlands (and a modern replica) hanging from the beams of the church, not to mention an inlaid marble table which illustrates the skill of the former craftsmen in Ashford marble. Queen Victoria, who had an affection for Whitby jet and Ashford marble, popularised the products of this village and specimens are now greatly prized in museums and private collections.

The end of June and beginning of July sees an upsurge of well-dressing activity, for screens are concurrently being prepared and put on display in four villages. Youlgreave inaugurated the custom about 1829 when the circular stone tank known as the Fountain was erected by public subscription to supply the residents with water. The Fountain was prominent in scenes from the T. E. Lawrence film, "The Virgin and the Gipsy", although its presence was purely incidental. Youlgreave screens maintain a high standard of technique and one of its dressers, Mr. Oliver Shimwell, has gone out as missionary to pioneer the custom in Stoney Middleton and Tideswell where he has held appointments in the teaching profession, and also at Wormhill, of which village his wife is a native.

Under the supervision of Mr. Shimwell, the Tideswell panel of dressers has varied Biblical events with architectural scenes and these are always superb in draughtsmanship, composition and choice of colour. Scenes depicting Westminster Abbey and St. Paul's Cathedral have been created in Tideswell and conveyed by road to these national shrines and there erected to raise funds for their renovation. For many years, only one screen was displayed in Fountain Square, but the custom is now given a wider application to permit others to demonstrate their skill in this floral art. Tideswell, of course, once had an ebbing and flowing well in Manchester Road, but it no longer fluctuates with the tidal action of the distant sea.

Litton, a daughter parish of Tideswell, joined the unofficial Guild of Well Dressers in 1969 and has made rapid progress in the art. Like the workers in the parent township, the Litton dressers have concentrated on several architectural subjects and achieved most creditable results.

Also celebrating the custom at this time is the village of Hope. Seth Evans (*Bradwell: Ancient and Modern*) writes that well-dressings were formerly held in this village, and one wonders whether Hope may have seen something of the early manifestation of the custom by pagan padres of the Roman soldiers based at nearby Navio (Brough), for some writers contend that the occupying forces of Rome may have introduced the doctrine of venerating water. The custom was revived in its present form in 1949.

A week later, Bakewell—famous for its puddings and its shows —carries on the custom. Like Tideswell, Bradwell and other names ending with the same suffix, it is commendable that Bakewell should thus (perhaps innocently and unconsciously) acknowledge its healing wells, even though the premises in Bath Street have been converted to other uses. It also has a Peat Well or/and Holy Well, where forgotten miracles of healing may have taken place. A swimming bath was erected in 1697 and was 33 ft. in length, 19 ft. in width, and with an arched stone roof. The temperature of the water was 59 degrees, but the optimism of an early writer was misplaced when he predicted: "In all probability these waters will some day become famous, and their value greatly appreciated."

Buxton—"Aquis" or "Aquae" of the Romans—has its reputation for healing waters, and its well-dressings take place the same time as at Bakewell. Buxton dressed its St. Ann's Well as far back as 1840, but there are some who postulate the theory that the dedication is mistaken, and that the inscription on an ancient statue was mis-read as St. Ann, whereas it may have been a mutilated form of Arnemeza, a pagan nymph who gave the settlement its name of Aquis Arnemeza or Aquae Arnemetia. The desecrated statue was found in the well and removed, along with shifts, shirts, crutches and offerings of wax by Sir William Bassett, a zealous Puritan. The well had a reputation for healing in those days and was sometimes known as the Holy Well, but the Puritans had no time for alleged miracles and little knowledge that certain minerals had curative and medicinal values.

Last century, it was not unusual to see "love feast" or "camp meeting" advised on the preaching plans of Methodist circuits; but they are now forgotten features of religious folk-lore. Mow Cop in Cheshire was renowned as the site of annual love feasts held under the auspices of the Primitive Methodist Connexion, and members gathered to share the communion of bread and water and give testimony to their work and witness for the Church. Love feasts are relics of one of the earliest observances of the Church and were known as the Feast of Agapae (the Greek word for the purest form of love), and the Christians met for fellowship and a communion of bread and water as a means of strengthening their mutual faith during times of severe persecution. Pictures showing this ancient ceremony may be seen painted on the walls of the Catacombs beneath Rome.

For some centuries this custom has been observed at Alport Castles Farm, a remote farm in the Woodlands where Methodism prospered last century. John Longden, landlord of the Snake Inn, was a renowned evangelical preacher and held prayer-meetings at the inn. The Duke of Devonshire had such admiration and esteem for his Methodist tenants that he built them their little wayside chapel. Each year on the first Sunday in July, faithful Methodists have gathered at this farm to share a simple repast of plum-cake and water to remind the present generation that they keep alive the faith of their forefathers in this feast of love and service.

Derbyshire has two Pilsleys, but it is the one near Chatsworth which incorporates well-dressing with a village fair during the middle of July. During the year of the Great Exhibition (1851), a visitor described the occasion when "there were nine carts or wagons of all shapes and sizes containing boys and girls from Eyam school, with their daddies and mammas, uncles and aunties, brothers and sisters, cousins and friends; a few flags, and headed by some stout fellows armed with cornopeans and trombones, blowing discordant sounds and making day hideous. Behind the two taps that supplied the village were erected the big screens, one twenty feet square. This wore the Duke of Devonshire's Arms, and a great variety of devices and mottoes. Shells were used. Branches of trees were at the side, and in front of the screen there was a miniature garden laid out with tiny gravel walks, flower beds with shell borders, and surrounded by a fence of ropes and sticks . . ."

Stoney Middleton has its festival on the old August Bank Holiday and the situation of the two wells near the church is ideal—except for the motorist who has difficulty in finding ways of access and egress. This village has its healing well thought to have been found or popularised by the Romans, and tradition claims that a Crusader, having contracted leprosy in the Holy Land was healed by bathing in its tepid waters, building the original church in thanksgiving for his recovery. There were formerly baths for both sexes which were built by the eccentric 2nd Lord Denman who lived at the Hall. The church, with its 15th century tower and octagonal nave of the 18th century, is an architectural curiosity well worth a visit. The custom was started in 1936 when Mr. Oliver Shimwell was headmaster of the school and, after his departure, was carried on under the leadership of the late Mr. B. Milner and a team of supporters. A novel frame, resembling the type used for oil paintings, was introduced for the children's well, and suggested the work of an old master.

About the same time of year, the Bonsall dressers erect their screens. The custom was revived in the Jubilee Year (1935) and one example was a portrait of King George V and Queen Mary.

In the church is a large stone ball to which is attached the iron bull-ring, relic of the barbarous customs of bull and bear baiting. At Chesterfield, before a bull was slaughtered, it had to be baited to make the meat tender. Failure to comply resulted in a fine. Also in the church, carved on a pillar which hides it from the pulpit, is the notorious Bonsall Imp.

From the year of its revival in 1949, Bradwell has continued the custom as the central attraction of its Gala Week held on the old August Bank Holiday. Here again, in the name of this village, we have the suffix "well" and not far from the point where Bathamgate cuts through the ancient Grey Ditch is a well which was so much esteemed for the treatment of scrofula and other skin diseases, that it was formerly sent away in barrels for the treatment of such complaints.

Barlow has its dressings in mid-August on the Wednesday following St. Lawrence's Day (August 14th). The custom here dates from 1840 and commemorates the installation of a public water supply. The method of "blossoming" the wells is favoured to that of "petalling" and the screens are presented in triptych style beneath canvas canopies. R. M. Gilchrist modelled the well-dressings in his novel "Willowbrake" on those at Barlow and Cutthorpe. Not far away, Marsh End has its well-dressing week towards the end of June.

Rush-bearing is now only a ghost which haunts the civil parish records of Derbyshire as well as those of an ecclesiastical character. We find references to rush carts and the rushes (sometimes hay) which were scattered as floor coverings for houses and churches. The sheaves of rushes, harvested and dried in marshy places, were ornamented with flowers and trinkets for their journey to church.

At the end of August, in the villages of Wormhill and Eyam, the summer series of well-dressings is brought to a close. At Eyam the festival integrates with the Wakes and annual Plague commemoration service, and provides a bonus attraction to visitors on this occasion. The Eyam festival was revived at the Festival of Britain and special screens include Plague Tercentenary pictures and one for the visit to Sheffield of the British Association for the Advancement of Science.

At Wormhill the subject is designed by Mr. O. Shimwell and the screen erected at the Brindley Well; memorial to the canal engineer, James Brindley, who was born in the parish in 1716. This fountain, where water was supplied for both man and beast, provides an ideal setting for the floral screen and also recalls the further use to which water has been applied — the needs of industry and transport.

2.   Shrovetide and Easter Customs

THE ringing of the Pancake Bell at 11-00 a.m. on Shrove Tuesday is a custom which has been supplanted in some villages by the running of Pancake Races, although these comparatively recent innovations have achieved only a limited popularity. At Ashbourne this once important day in the Church calendar is marked by a secular activity—the communal game of football. This long established custom originated at Derby where it fell into decay and was subsequently adopted at Ashbourne. Its origin is claimed to date back to the Roman occupation, which should surely make Derby the birthplace of this now internationally popular sport. The first "match of the day" is said to have taken place in 217 AD when Roman legionaries, on their way to nearby Derventio, marched imperiously through the site which was later occupied by Saxon "Northworthy" and Danish "Derby". Provoked by the haughtiness of the troops, the local population drove them out with a great slaughter, and their triumph was afterwards made the subject of annual celebration.

The game was developed with a minimum of rules and restrictions, and these were made flexible enough to suit the convenience of the players, providing a capital way in which the participants might settle old grievances or create new ones. The opposing teams consisted of all able-bodied parishioners of St. Peter's, whose goal was at Gallows Balk on the Normanton road, and All Saints' residents defended a goal at Nun's Mill. The "centre" was the market-place where the ball was tossed into the eager crowd. "This is seized upon by some of the strongest and most active men of each party. The rest of the players immediately close in upon them, and a solid mass is formed. It then becomes the object of each party to impel the course of the crowd towards their particular goal. The struggle to obtain the ball, which is carried in the arms of those who have possessed themselves of it, is then violent, and the motion of this human tide heaving to and fro, without the least regard for consequences, is tremendous. Broken shins, broken heads, torn coats and lost hats, are among the minor accidents of this fearful contest, and it frequently happens that persons fall in consequence of the intensity of the pressure, fainting and bleeding beneath the feet of the surrounding mob ... The object of the St. Peter's party is to get the ball into the water, down the Morledge Brook into the Derwent as soon as they can, while the All Saints' party endeavour to prevent this, and to urge the ball westward. The St. Peter players are considered to be equal to the best water-spaniels, and it is certainly curious to see two or three hundred men up to their chins in the Derwent continually ducking each other. The numbers engaged on both sides exceed a thousand, and the streets are crowded with lookers on. The shops are closed, and the town presents the aspect of a place suddenly taken by storm."

Stephen Glover, who supplied this information in 1829, also says: — "A desperate game at football, in which the ball is struck by the feet of the players, is also played at Ashover and at other wakes."

The ball at Derby was made of leather stuffed with shavings and was thrown into the crowd from the Town Hall. The man who succeeded in "scoring" was acknowledged champion for the year and was chaired through the streets of the town to the accompaniment of the church bells. The bells of the five different churches were always rung in the morning and an old jingle recalls the custom:

> *Pancakes and fritters*
> *Say All Saints' and St. Peter's;*
> *When will the ball come*
> *Say the bells of St. Alkmund;*
> *At two they will throw,*
> *Says Saint Werebo';*
> *Oh, very well,*
> *Says little Michel.*

When or why this riotous custom was transferred to Ashbourne does not appear to be known, but it provoked the same zeal and enthusiasm, and caused the same indiscriminate damage to people and property in this town as it had done at Derby. It was well established in 1821 for a comedian named Fawcett composed and sang a ballad in Ashbourne Theatre during that year, of which the following two verses are of more particular interest to the student of folk-lore.

> *Shrove Tuesday, you know, is always the day,*
> *When pancake's the prelude, and Foot-ball's the play,*
> *Where upwards and downwards men ready for fun,*
> *Like the French at the Battle of Waterloo run.*
> *And well may they run like the devil to pay,*

15

'Tis always the case as I have heard say,
If a Derbyshire Foot-ball man comes in the way,
In the neat little town of Ashbourne.

The ball is turn'd up and the Bull Ring's the place,
And as fierce as a bull-dog's is every man's face;
Whilst kicking and shouting and howling they run,
Until every stitch in the Ball come's undone.
There's Faulkner and Smith, Bodge Hand and some more,
Who hide it and hug it and kick it so sore,
And deserve a good whopping at every man's door
In the neat little town of Ashbourne.

Strenuous attempts were made to suppress the game, but the residents resisted every effort to achieve its outlawry. In 1860 several players were summoned by the police and sentenced by the magistrates. They appealed to the Court of the Queen's Bench, but lost their case. A circular entitled "Death of the Right Honourable Game Football" was distributed in Ashbourne, giving a satirical account of the decease of the game, but threatening its resurrection the following year. The account concluded with an epitaph:

May Liberty meet with success,
    May Prudence protect her from evil:
But may tyrants and tyranny tine* in the mist,
    And wander their way to the Devil.
*Tine: Kindle.

In spite of the apparent victory of the town authorities, the ball was "turned up" in the market-place in 1862, but a formal pledge was given that the game should not be played in future in the streets of the town. It was afterwards transferred to a more innocuous, site, with Clifton Mill and Sturston Mill remaining as goals, but the game was set in motion in The Paddock.

The balls are made by Mr. Arthur Chadwick, an Ashbourne saddler, and his father, Mr. Percy Chadwick, made them for many years before. They are painted and enamelled to the design chosen by the celebrities who are invited to perform the inaugural ceremony of "turning up" the ball on Shrove Tuesday and Ash Wednesday.

Although some people suggest that Mothering, or Mid-Lent Sunday is of American origin and has a purely family significance, this is a custom dating back to the pre-Reformation faith. It was given this name in honour of the parent or Mother Church. when the epistle for the day was from Galatians, chapter IV, in

16

which we find the reference:— "But Jerusalem which is above is free, which is the mother of us all."

At Tideswell, the ancient ceremony of "clypping the church" was revived for a period and held on this day. Members of the daughter churches of Litton and Millers Dale joined with members of the parent church for a united service, following which they encircled the church, holding hands and singing: "We love the place O God, wherein Thine honour dwells". A similar custom was observed at Wirksworth. Tideswell was formerly ringed with stone crosses set up at points where parishioners from outlying parts might catch their first glimpse of the pinnacles of the ancient "Cathedral of the Peak". The hollow base of one near Wheston is still to be seen by the wayside, but passing years have re-named it the Wishing Well. Butterton Cross plinth is built into the foundations of a wall skirting the old road from Millers Dale, while Poynton Cross and Summer Cross exist purely as place-names.

Castleton people used to climb a hill behind their village on Easter Sunday morning to watch the sun rise, because it was reputed to dance on this day. The superstition is thought to stem from Druid practice. There is a natural explanation to such a phenomenon which may be due to refraction as the rays of the sun filter through the morning mist.

People living in the vicinity of Deepdale were in the habit of paying pilgrimage to a spring near Hob's Hurst Cave, the water of which was supposed to be charmed by a goblin which inhabited the cave. Mortals who drank from the spring on Good Friday morning were healed of their complaints, which seems a strange medieval mixture of pagan and Christian belief.

On Easter Sunday morning, children from Ashford-in-the-Water visited a grotto at the foot of Great Shacklow Wood known as the Sinner's Well. They were each provided with a cup and a quarter pound of sugar which they dissolved in water from the spring and drank on the spot. Tideswell children went to the Dropping Tor spring and sweetened the water they caught in their cups with sugar. The ritual was known as "sugar-cupping" and was carried out in many other villages.

It is possible that the "shake-bottles" supplied to children on Easter Monday developed from sugar-cupping. At Stoney Middleton the children filled their bottles at Billy Brewer's Well, to which they added a compound of crushed boiled sweets, mints, liquorice, and other confections. This mixture was shaken vigorously until the ingredients were dissolved and produced a tasty froth which was sipped with relish. As the contents of the bottle became steadily reduced, more water was added at intervals, until the liquid was much weakened and diminished in flavour. This beverage no doubt had a certain medical value and

17

would help to minimise coughs, colds and throat infections prevalent at that time of the year.

At Buxton, Easter Monday and Tuesday were days when the custom of "lifting" was carried out. At Bradwell the practice was called "cucking", which was another name for "kissing". Groups of males went round on the Monday with a chair in which they claimed the privilege of lifting members of the fair sex, afterwards requiring a kiss or small forfeit. The following day, the ladies were at liberty to retaliate, but on both days the custom ceased at noon. The wide popularity of the custom was noted by a Manchester correspondent to *The Gentleman's Magazine* for February, 1784. He wrote that " 'lifting' was originally designed to represent our Saviour's Resurrection. The men lift the women on Easter Monday and the women the men on Easter Tuesday. One or more take hold of each leg, and one or more each arm near the body, and lift the person up in a horizontal position, three times. It is a rude, indecent, and dangerous diversion, practised chiefly by the lower class of people. Our magistrates constantly prohibit it by the bellman, but it subsists at the end of the town; and the women have of late years converted it into a money job. I believe it is chiefly confined to these northern counties."

The religious significance was that the person was lifted three times and this denoted the three days and nights in which Jesus lay in the tomb, and the cheering was to mark the triumph of His resurrection. Like many debased customs, it had strayed far from its religious origins and no one now knows the purpose for which it was observed.

In a record from the Tower of London there is a reference to the taking of Edward Longshanks in his bed by a party of ladies of the bedchamber and maids of honour, on Easter Monday, for "the purpose of heaving or lifting the king, on the authority of a custom which then doubtless prevailed among all ranks throughout the kingdom". In Shropshire, Cheshire and Lancashire, those who were too modest to submit to the kiss were fined a shilling, and given a written testimony exempting them from further molestation.

Dr. S. O. Addy wrote that "Cucking was a very rough practice, and it sometimes led to charges of assault being made before the magistrates. At Castleton it was sometimes done by putting a 'fork stale' or fork handle under the girl's legs and lifting her up. It required two young men to do this. More frequently two men seized a girl by the arms and shoulders, tossed her up, and caught her as she fell."

The same writer says:— "At Bradwell and Castleton parents tell their children to put pins into wells on Palm Sunday, or if they fail to do so they will break their bottles (shake-bottles) on the following Easter Monday. The pins must be new and straight, not crooked. I have talked to children who have done this, and one of them, a girl of about fourteen years old, said the children go in great numbers on the afternoon of Palm Sunday to a well in Bradwell, behind Micklow. The Bradwell children used to drop pins on this day into a well in Charlotte Lane, and also into a pond between Bradwell and Brough. Mr. Robert Bradwell, of Bradwell, aged 88, told me that on Palm Sunday 'the children used to put new pins into lady wells, and the lady of the well would not let them have clean water until they did that'. There is a lady well at the back of the castle at Castleton, from which the children used to fill their bottles at Easter, and there is another at Great Hucklow from which they filled their bottles. Mr. Bradwell said the object of the children was to get clean water by the lady's influence".

These childhood customs again seem to be a compound of pagan and Christian superstition, for the "lady wells" were thought to be under the influence of elves who could be placated by the offering of pins, although the name suggests they may have been holy wells dedicated to the Virgin Mary in the first place.

On Shrove Tuesday the custom of "Besom Stale" was carried out at Tideswell when children late for school were carried shoulder high on the stale of a broom or besom, and in later years on a pole or cart-shaft, by their fellow pupils who sang:

> *We dar ner bar him aght,*
> *We dar ner bar him aght,*
> *For he's a jolly good fellow,*
> *An' so say all on us.*

It was also the practice to lock the schoolmaster out of school until the children had extracted the promise of a holiday. On arrival at school he was greeted from behind the bolted door with the chant:

> *Pardon, mister, pardon,*
> *Pardon in a spoon,*
> *If you don't give us a holiday*
> *We'll bar you out till noon.*

19

3. The Merry Month of May

"MAY-DAY" was once a magic word. Now it has no more significance for many people than any other normal day of the year. It was a day when the coming of springtime was welcomed by many demonstrations of joy. Housewives hung out bunches of flowers from their cottage windows and children wove the coloured ribbons of the maypole into such intricate patterns as the Gipsy's Tent and Spider's Web. Carters and carriers paid extra attention to the grooming of their horses, plaiting coloured ribbons into their manes and tails as well as adorning them with highly polished brasses which glinted in the sunlight. These appear to have been charms or talismans, and were similar to the crescents and other adornments worn by camels in the Middle East.

In some villages it was the custom to anoint sick and weakly children with freshly gathered May-dew; a custom said to derive from Druid practice, although it also recalls the Biblical injunction for elders of the Early Church to anoint its sick members with oil as a supplement to the prayer of faith. William Wood, the Eyam chronicler, states: — "One of the incantations practised at the festival of the Druids was to anoint the forehead of a sick person with May-dew, which was carefully gathered at daybreak, and the cure, of course, immediately followed. Now at Eyam and in its vicinity it was once a general, and in some measure is still a prevailing custom, to anoint weak and diseased children with May-dew."

May-dew was also highly esteemed as an astringent. Samuel Pepys made an entry in his diary: — "My wife away down with Jane and W. Hewer to Woolwich, in order to a little ayre, and to lie there to-night, and so to gather May-dew to-morrow morning, which Mrs. Turner hath taught her is the only thing in the world to wash her face with; and I am contented with it." An article in *The Morning Post* for 1791 reported that "yesterday being the 1st of May, according to annual and superstitious custom, a number of persons went into the fields and bathed their faces with the dew on the grass, under the idea that it would render them beautiful." An old ballad says: —

Vain hope! No more in choral bands unite
Her virgin votaries, and at early dawn
Sacred to May and Love's mysterious rites,
Brush the light dew-drops from the spangled lawn.

J. B. Firth (*Highways and Byways of Derbyshire*) mentions a May-day custom at Eyam, although I have never found any supporting reference made by William Wood, or other writers. He describes it as "a species of Morris dance, indulged in on May Day. The inhabitants of the first house in the village began it by taking hands and dancing to the second house. There they were joined by their neighbours and danced together to the third, until the whole long street of Eyam was full of the dancing throng."

Reference will be found elsewhere to the custom of kit-dressing performed at Baslow Wakes. An old writer says:— "On the 1st of May, and the five and six days following, all the pretty young country girls that serve the town with milk dress themselves up very neatly, and borrow abundance of silver plate, whereof they make a pyramid, which they adorn with ribbands and flowers, and carry upon their heads, instead of their common milk-pails. In this equipage, accompany'd by some of their fellow milk-maids, and a bagpipe or fiddle, they go from door to door, dancing before the houses of their customers, in the midst of boys and girls that follow them in troops, and everybody gives them something."

An old ballad entitled "The Milk Maid's Life", printed in 1630, runs as follows:—

Upon the first of May,
With garlands fresh and gay,
With mirth and musick sweet,
For such a season meet,
They passe their time away;
They dance away sorrow,
And all the day thorow
Their legs doe never fayle.
They nimbly their feet do ply,
And bravely try the victory
In honour o' th' milhing paile.

May 13th was the occasion of the annual festival of the lead miners. On this day they dressed their coes—the structure at the top of their shafts—and ore-houses, with oak branches, garlands and other rustic decorations. They enjoyed a solid dinner of beef, pudding and ale provided, if the weather permitted, in the open air. The Bar-master presided and the day ended with folksongs and music. The last dinner was held at Wirksworth in 1870 when 120 miners were entertained at the expense of Mr. E. M. Wass, of Lea.

The lead-miners had their own exclusive code of laws, customs and privileges which were framed and enforced for many centuries by the barmote courts which probably date back to Saxon times. These ancient laws were looked upon with royal and religious favour because of the revenues accruing to both Church and State. For many years they largely existed in the form of a 17th century poem composed by Edward Manlove, of Wirksworth; a technique adopted in order that the largely illiterate miners might memorise the privileges and rights to which they were entitled. In 1852 legislation was introduced to regulate such largely verbal enactments and embody them in an Act of Parliament. The arbitrary courts for the several Liberties, or areas of lead-mining operation, may still be invoked to ratify claims or settle disputes relating to the industry. Jurymen of the courts meet annually for formal appointment, and these occasions are concluded with a traditional dinner provided at the expense of the Lords of the Mineral Field, who represent the interests of the Crown.

The third Sunday in May was known in Derbyshire at one time as Sugar and Water Sunday when young women provided sugar and water for members of the opposite sex. The compliment was returned by the young men treating the girls to ale, cakes and punch at public-houses.

Other Maytime activities have been referred to elsewhere and include Rogationtide services at Staveley; the well-dressings at Tissington; and the Castleton Garland ceremony.

4. The Castleton Garland

"STRANGERS who have observed in books of travel pictures of the High Peak cavern, are inclined to wonder what the weird, gallows-like uprights and posts are, with flying ropes and hanging weights, with adjacent suggestions of vast wheels and curious figures standing out against the darkness. This is the ropery. Each master has his walk. Seven rope-walks traverse the stupendous excavation which is the hallway of the so-called Devil's Hole, with its headways and subways, its halls of Eblis and its dripping wells, its underground rivers and its other mysteries beyond ..."

"Mr. Ruskin probably never saw this High Peak house of labour. Otherwise the world would have heard something of it, since the recluse of the Lakes loves hand-made things, and delights in the primitive, the lowly, and the natural. The ropers of the Peak, who pay no rent and work in a factory made by God, spin and weave in the old Egyptian way. Their ropes and twine, their halters and clothes-lines, their whipcord and cables, are all made by hand. Their factory has no doors. It is open to sun and shadow, to summer winds and winter blasts, and the ropers work there right through the year. It is a sheltered site. You arrive at it through a valley which is made musical by the brook that is born in the cavern and which now and then becomes a torrent—angry, yellow, opaque, terrible ..."

So wrote Joseph Hatton in *The Banishment of Jessop Blythe* when describing the dead industry of making ropes at Castleton. Even though it is dead, the wooden skeleton of the rope-walk still rouses the curiosity of visitors to the Peak Cavern, and fortunately, Mr. C. Marrison, last of the ropemakers, has been filmed more than once carrying out the techniques of this ancient industry.

For centuries the cottages, inns and church of Castleton have grovelled at the foot of Peveril Castle, acknowledging their allegiance to this venerable monarch seated upon a throne of towering limestone, moodily surveying the valley and its encircling hills, perhaps thinking of the palmy days when jousting knights fought their tournaments. It was here that Guaine de Metz, a knight of Lorraine, with his maiden shield of silver and peacock crest, vanquished many knights—including a prince of Scotland and a knight of Burgoyne—to win the hand of Mellet, elder daughter of Pain Peverel, and her dowry of Whittington Castle in Shropshire.

The limestone hills, bare and barren, grim and cold though they may appear, have proved rich in mineral treasure, providing a prosperous livelihood to lead and fluorspar miners and the lapidaries who work the exquisitely coloured Blue John into attractive ornaments, vases and jewellery which beguile the pockets and purses of the tourists who throng its crooked streets, explore its gloomy caverns, and visit its museum and ancient church.

Every Oak Apple Day (29th May), unless it happens to be a Sunday, Castleton observes a now unique custom. This is the Garland ceremony. Seth Evans (*Bradwell: Ancient and Modern*) speaks of the custom being carried out in the neighbouring villages of Bradwell and Hope, as it was in many parts of the country in past days. R. M. Gilchrist wrote:— "Castleton is famous for a pageant which is performed every Royal Oak Day. Then gaily-dressed children dance what survives of the Morris, and the village band plays its best; whilst King Charles and his lady wife, acted by two Peaklanders of the sterner sex, ride in state through the quaint streets. His majesty, in cavalier costume, has the upper part of his body covered with a gorgeous bouqet, in shape not unlike a beehive, which, towards evening, is drawn up to the top of the church tower, and left to wither upon a pinnacle."

The garland is constructed on a frame which nowadays incorporates a bicycle wheel rim and hoops of plywood decorated with garden and field flowers. The garland is crowned with a special knot of flowers known as the "queen". When complete it weighs about six stones and measures three feet in height. The six village inns take turns in making the garland and the procession starts from the particular inn where it has been made, but actually begins its tour of the village from Squires Lane. In former days, a male team of Morris dancers performed to the music of "th' puddin' baked i' a lantern" tune played by the village band. Dancers used to hum a doggerel rhyme to the tune and this helped them to remember the various steps and movements of the dance. Part of the verse runs:—

> *Ah dunna know, Ah dunna care,*
> *What they do i' Bradda:*
> *Piece o' beef an' a owd cow's yeead,*
> *An' a puddin' baked i' a lantern.*

Some writers have contended that the music is a survival of the Helston Floral Dance tune, arguing that it was introduced by a contingent of Cornish miners who came to help drive the Grand Navigation canal in the Speedwell Mine. But this seems scarcely feasible as the words of that song do not match up to the metre of the Castleton verse quoted above.

The main characters in the pageant are the King, whose head and shoulders are covered by the flower-smothered garland, and his consort, both of whom ride on shire horses. They were formerly accompanied by several courtiers dressed in costume of the Stuart period, while another man preceded the party and his duty consisted of sweeping the road with a besom. Until 1955, a male masqueraded as Queen, but the role is now played with the greater grace and dignity of the gentler sex and with less of the buffoonery which marked the parades of past days.

When the procession has halted at the various inns for refreshment, and the children have performed their dance, it is finally disbanded at the foot of the church tower (decorated with oak branches for the occasion) and there the King is relieved of his stifling burden. This is then attached to a pulley and hauled up to be secured to a pinnacle of the tower where it is left to shrivel and decay. The special posy, or "queen", which surmounted the garland, is then taken and laid on the nearby village war memorial and the Last Post is sounded as a tribute to the memory of the men of Castleton who never returned from the two world wars. After a Maypole display by the children, parents wearing oak sprays sometimes join with them in dancing through the streets.

A former vicar of Castleton objected to the garland being hung from the church tower on the grounds that the custom was of pagan origin and reflected the worship and sacrificial rites of the Druids performed in groves of oak. It has also been claimed to be a development of the "Green Man" figure symbolising the growth of crops, but to the layman it seems more likely to be a masque celebrating the Restoration of Charles II on the 29th May, 1660, and more particularly his escape after the Battle of Worcester when he lay concealed in the Boscobel Oak.

Until 1897 the practice was carried out by the bell-ringers and in the Churchwardens' Accounts (1749) there is an entry: — "For an iron Rod to hang ye ringers Garland in ... 8d." Some have mis-read the entry as "singer's garland", suggesting that it may have been the choristers who observed the custom, but it is established that the ceremony gave opportunity for the ringers to be publicly rewarded for their services to the parish. Collections are now devoted to other charities.

5.   The Whitsun Ales

LIKE several other ancient ecclesiastical observances, that of the Whitsun Ales appears to have either outlived its usefulness or has long been suppressed because of abuses which developed during the attendant revelries. The ceremonies attaching to this particular custom seem to have been altogether of a secular character and quite devoid of any spiritual significance. They were simply designed to raise revenue for the church and parish, and also to meet the frequent appeals—known as "briefs"—which were circulated from time to time to solicit contributions towards the relief of townships or individuals overtaken by misfortune or disaster. In some respects the Whitsun Ales were precursors of the rating system and met a variety of needs by a more voluntary method of levy. They also provided yet another excuse for banquets which were so popular on "holy days".

Some writers maintain that the custom was a degenerate survival of the early Christian "agapae", or love feast. By some warped misinterpretation of theological teaching, it was argued that participants in these sometimes promiscuous forms of roistering would be absolved from guilt of any moral misdemeanours or indulgence in any otherwise inexcusable excesses, by the fact that they were making donations to some worthy charity. Therefore fasting was followed by feasting and worship by wantonness on the assumption that "according to the christian rule, all festivities were rendered innocent by alms."

In 1570, William Kethe bitterly complained that these revellings had not only desecrated the sabbath days but had degenerated into "bulbeatings, bearebeatings, bowlings, dicying, cardyng, daunsynges, diunkenness, and whoredome, in so much, as men could not keepe their servauntes from lyinge out of theyr owne houses the same Sabbath-day at night."

Churchwardens organised the occasion by collecting malt from parishioners for brewing the beer. Having made their contribution they were then entitled to share in the refreshment they had helped to provide. The churchwardens rivalled each other in a spirit of friendly competition as to whom could make the largest profit. Stubbs, in his *Anatomie of Abuses*, describes this ancient custom as follows: "In certaine townes, where dronken Bacchus beares swaie, against Christmas and Easter, Whitsondaie, or some other tyme, the churchewardens of every parishe, with the consent of the whole parishe, provide halfe a score or twentie quarters of mault, whereof some they buy of the churche stocke, and some is given them of the parishioners themselves, every one conferring somewhat, according to his abilitie; whiche maulte being made into very strong ale or bere, is sette to sale, either in the church or some other place assigned to that purpose. Then when this is set abroche, well is he that can gete the soonist to it, and spend the most at it. In this kinde of practice they continue sixe weekes, a quarter of a yeare, yea, half a yeare together. That money, they say, is to repaire their churches and chappels with, to buy bookes for service, cuppes for the celebration of the Sacrament, surplesses for sir John, and such other necessaries. And they maintaine other extraodinarie charges in their parish besides."

The ceremonies were presided over by a young couple elected at a public meeting to be the lord and lady of the ale, and they dressed as suitably as their circumstances could afford to fulfil the role with due dignity and with deference to tradition. Sometimes the expense incurred by these central characters would be subsidised from church funds as in 1621 when an entry was made:— "Paid to her that was Lady at Whitsontide by consent ... 5s. od."

An empty barn or other suitable building was adapted as the "lord's hall" where the populace were entertained to a substantial repast. The lord and lady were attended by a steward, sword-bearer, purse-bearer and mace-bearer, each carrying the appropriate emblem of office, while there was a train-bearer or page, and a jester who entertained the assembly with his antics. The mace was made of silk, finely plaited, with ribbands on top, and filled with spices and perfumes. Music was supplied for dancing by a pipe and tabor, and often Morris-dancers provided entertainment. This aspect of the custom was thought to have been introduced as a means of perpetuating the Drink-lean, a festival observed by tenants and vassals of the lord of the fee within his manor. Another ramification of the custom was the erection of arbors in church-yards when the presiding characters were Robin Hood and Maid Marian.

Stephen Glover has a record of the Whitsun Ales being celebrated in the south of Derbyshire, although it was no doubt commonly practised in other parishes. He wrote:—

"In Dodsworth's manuscripts, in the Bodleian library, there is the following record. 'The inhabitants of Elvaston and Ockbrook were formerly required by mutual agreement to brew four ales, and every ale of one quarter of malt, and at their own costs and charges, betwixt this and the feast of St. John the baptist next coming. And every inhabitant of Ockbrook shall be at the several ales, and every husband and wife were to pay two-pence, every cottager one penny, and all the inhabitants of the said towns of Elvaston, Thurlaston and Ambaston, shall have and receive all the profits and advantages, coming of the said ales, to the use and behoof of the said church of Elvaston; and the inhabitants of the said towns of Elvaston, Thurlaston and Ambaston, shall brew eight ales betwixt this and the feast of St. John the baptist, at which ales, and every one of them, the inhabitants shall come and pay as before rehearsed, who, if he be away at one ale to pay at the t'oder ale for both, or else send his money. And the inhabitants of Ockbrook shall carry all manner of tymber, being in the Dale wood now felled, that the said priest chyrch of the said town of Elvaston, Thurlaston and Ambaston shall occupy to the use of the said church.' This appears to be the ancient method of paying money for the repair of country churches.''

6.   The Gospel Mine

SOME of the names of old Derbyshire lead-mines are so picturesque and descriptive that they could have been christened by poets, painters or preachers. Just think of a few:— Dream, Silver Hillock, Green Leys, Shining Gutter, Bluebell, Cowslip, Daisy Rake, Brightside, Glad Rake, Green Linnets, Robin-wash, Bird's Nest, Strawberry Lees, Providence, God-be-here, Glory, Ranter, Virgin, St. Mary's, Buy-the-Truth, Never Fear, Daily Bread and Paradise.

Others are much more sinister and remind us of the names given to their mines by prospectors in the Wild West—Brimstone Dyke, Burnt Heath, Brandy Bottle, Carrion Hole, Bacchus Pipe, Raper, Hell Rake, Silence, Black Hole, Thunder-pit, Cursed Moor, Cackle Mackle, Nickalum, Maury, Bundog and Fiery Dragon. Some could be the names of race-horses:— Smiling Fancy, Lucky Ploughman, Speed, Speedwell, Merlin and Good Luck. Some remind us of the personal hazards and financial risks of the miner's occupation:— Hazard, Venture, Pot Luck, Providence, Perseverance, Long-looked-for, Found-at-last, Victory and Have-it-all. The story concerning the last named mine is that a prospector had exhausted all his capital in an unsuccessful speculation. Among his few remaining possessions was an aged cockerel which he took to the mine and, flinging the protesting bird down the shaft, he exclaimed in disgust—"Here, have it aw!"

Another mine called Watch and Ward recalls the site at which the former civil custom of keeping watch and ward at the main entrance to a village was observed. Such place-names as Lydgate, Lidgett (cover-gate) and Tenter Lane (watch-lane) recall this same custom. A rota of all able bodied men in the community was drawn up and they took turns to keep watch from dusk to daylight. Armed with a watch-bill and lantern, these men were stationed at the main approach to a village and were entrusted with the security of the township. It was their duty to challenge and ascertain the business of any stranger seeking admission to the village during the hours of darkness, and so the rest of the population were able to sleep without fear of molestation to their persons or property. When the sentry had completed his vigil, he took his watch-bill and lantern and left them beside the door of his successor.

The name of one mine has always intrigued me, although the site is only marked by broken walls and a few mounds of grass-covered mineral. It is called the Gospel Mine and is situated just off the road connecting Calver Sough with Hassop. But why Gospel Mine? How did it acquire such an unusual name? Was it given the name during some religious revival or by some devout evangelical? Or could it have been because tithes were paid by lead-miners to the Church and the clergy were therefore under obligation to pray for their protection and prosperity? This was hardly the reason, for the miners greatly resented the imposition of such an unfair tax and much money was spent in legal opposition to its payment. There was a Ranter Mine, of course, and "ranter" was a nickname given to the pioneers of Primitive Methodism because of their faith and fervour. But none of these suggestions give any hint to help elucidate the mystery of the name "Gospel Mine", and we must look elsewhere for an explanation.

The answer to the riddle is supplied by an examination of the Ordnance Survey map of the district, for this mine is sited exactly on a boundary separating two parishes and the prefix is quite simply explained by the fact that prayers were recited at this point during the former Rogation services. This rural custom was carried out by clergy and parishioners when "perambulating" the boundaries of their parish in order that prayers might be offered at intervals for the prosperity of the growing crops and with the plea that the population might be preserved from pestilence, famine, drought and other calamities common in past days.

Looking still further afield, we find that there is a Gospel Stone in the village of Hathersage. This consists of a worn sandstone boulder which projects slightly on to a footpath from the wall surrounding a council estate in the Dale. The boulder narrowly escaped destruction from workmen when it proved to be out of alignment with the wall they were building, but the Rev. J. H. Brooksbank, then Vicar of Hathersage, intervened and pointed out the significance of this ancient Rogation landmark. A plaque now draws attention to its presence and place in village history.

Near the village of Taddington we may find the Gospel Hillocks, a name given to prehistoric tumuli because of the part they formerly played as a halting place in the parish perambulation. Osmaston has a Gospel Greave Close, the rent of which formerly provided money disbursed as a village charity. Eyam had its now forgotten Gospel Places consisting of heaps of stone, as well as a site on the parish boundary still called the Old Oak

Tree, which is probably a corruption of Holy Oak Tree. Ashover had a Gospel Tree and Hayfield a Gospel Well, both place-names being attributed to the dubious claim that John Wesley preached at these respective sites. The number of places at which Wesley is claimed to have preached must far outnumber the apocryphal beds in which Queen Elizabeth is supposed to have slept. But Wesley did actually preach in Hayfield Church and made the following reference in his Journal for 23rd July, 1748, to terrible floods in the township "such as had not been seen by any living in those parts. Several water-mills and two women were swept away, part of the churchyard was torn up, and dead bodies washed away." It is far more likely that the names were given in connection with the springtime pilgrimage as priest and parishioners paused each year to make their act of worship. At Chapel-en-le-Frith there is a Gospel Brow where stood a tree which sheltered another famous preacher—the Rev. William Bagshawe, Apostle of the Peak. While not doubting or disputing that this is a genuine claim, it is feasible that the name was in existence in the above context long before the time of the famous 17th century evangelical.

Robert Plot in *The Natural History of Staffordshire* (1686) makes reference to a custom of adorning wells on 29th May with "boughs and flowers: this it seems they do at all gospel places whether wells, trees or hills ..."

Robert Herrick refers to Gospel Trees in his poem *Hesperides,* when he says: —

Dearest, bury me
Under that Holy-Oke, or Gospel Tree,
Where (though thou see'st me not), thou may'st think upon
Me, when thou yearly go'st procession.

Parish accounts suggest that these occasions incurred a charge on church funds and Hope Churchwardens' Accounts provide typical examples: —

"1688.	Spent in going with the perambulation ...	4s. 6d.
1690.	Spent of ye people yt went with the procession	£1 os. od.
1691.	Paid for Ale and Bread in going with Procession, which it is to be omitted for ye future till further order	9s. 3d.
1700.	Pd ye Clarke his wages £2. pd. him more for Ale drunk wn we went ye procession	13s. od.
		£2 13s. od."

A 17th century poet described the procession and its purpose as follows: —

That ev'ry man might keepe his owne possessions,
Our fathers us'd, in reverent processions,
(With zealous prayers, and with praiseful cheere),
To walke their parish-limits once a year:
And well-knowne markes (which sacrilegious hands
Now cut or breake) so border'd out their lands,
That ev'ry one distinctly knew his owne,
And many brawles, now rife, were then unknowne.

An old writer claimed that the custom was of pagan origin, and was "an imitation of the Feast called Terminalia, which was dedicated to the God Terminus, whom they considered as the guardian of fields and landmarks, and the keeper up of peace and friendship among men. The primitive custom used by the Christians on this occasion was for the people to accompany the bishop or some clergy into the fields, where litanies were made, and the mercy of God implored, that he would avert the evils of plague and pestilence, that he would send them good and seasonable weather, and give them in due season the fruits of the earth."

This religious ritual was also made the occasion of a ceremony of civil significance—that of "beating the bounds"—when the outlying points of the parish were visited for a different purpose. Most people were unable to read maps or written directions and so they walked along the hedges, streams, lanes, walls and fences which circumscribed their parish. In order to impress these boundaries upon the memory of the rising generation, children were whipped at strategic points, and, when they grew to manhood and became parents, they were able to pass on the knowledge so painfully acquired by administering the same ritual to their own offspring. At a harbour on the south coast, the children were pricked with pins for the same purpose.

The custom has been revived from time to time in several Derbyshire parishes, and I remember hearing of one rural parish where the pilgrimage took place each evening during Rogation week, with certain farms providing a tradition of hospitality for the blind clergyman and his parishioners as they toured the parish. It is currently carried out at Staveley where coal-fields jostle against corn-fields, and where the rural character of the parish has been much eroded by the spreading growth of its mammoth steel and chemical complex. But this parish, which keeps a burning lamp and a lump of coal on its church altar to remind worshippers of the cost of this product in terms of human life, still finds time to keep alive a custom which teaches us of the importance of food as well as of fuel and of the interdependence of industry and agriculture.

A large crowd watches the scramble for the ball during the Shrove Tuesday game of Ashbourne Football.

Ashbourne Footballs and their maker (Photos: Ashbourne Evening Telegraph).

The "king" of the Castleton Garland Ceremony (Sheffield Morning Telegraph).

Views of the Gospel Stone, Hathersage (J. Bricklebank).

A funeral garland at Ashford-in-the-Water church (John McCrindle).

7.

Garlands, Gloves and "Greensleeves"

WE usually associate the word "garland" with rejoicing, with the coloured paper chains which festoon our rooms at Christmas, or with the flags and bunting looped across the streets at carnival times. Or we may perhaps think of the huge garland of oak-leaves laced with flowers—with its obscure connection with King Charles II hiding in the Boscobel Oak—carried at Castleton on Garland Day.

But the garlands with which this chapter is concerned were symbols of sadness. Made in memory of maidens who died un-married, they were designed to illustrate the affection of her family and the sympathy of her friends. The flowers of which they were composed were intended to represent the fragrance and fragility of the spent life, and the use of white paper, silk, or similar material denoted the chastity of her living. Such garlands were made long before the first Elizabeth came to the throne, and feminine fingers were still weaving them during the reign of Queen Victoria, while at Abbot's St. Ann's in Dorset—where about forty virgins' crowns adorn the interior of the church, one was made as recently as 1953. The garlands hung like paper lanterns from the rafters of churches all over the country—the hatchments of simple, but sentimental people. They were land-marks of local history, reminding one generation of the tragedies and sorrows of another; reminding us of days different to our own; days when sorrow, entering one home in a village, entered almost every other, for the sorrow of one family touched so wide a circle of relatives, friends and neighbours, that it was shared by the whole closely knit community.

Dr. Spencer T. Hall, visiting Hathersage over a century ago, commended the custom and wrote:— "But one of the most interesting of all objects that catch the attention here is the sight of a number of withered chaplets and garlands within the church, hanging among the mouldered monuments and escutcheons, above some neglected tombs in the north aisle." Others have scoffed at the custom. After paying a visit to Tideswell Church about the year 1790, John Byng wrote in the *Torrington*

Diaries:— "They continue to hang up maiden garlands, which, however laudable as a tendency to virtue, will soon be laughed out of practice." It is rather to be regretted that this prophecy did come true, for only a few churches retain these interesting memorials of mourning. With the coming of new clergy or church wardens who condemned them as being morbid and conducive to melancholy, or with the restoration of the churches, the garlands were removed and thoughtlessly destroyed. Odd ones were rescued, as in the case of two acquired from Matlock Church a century ago by the antiquary, Thomas Bateman, who placed them in his museum for preservation. But more often than not the dusty and faded emblems were destroyed, and such entries as the one in Hope churchwarden's accounts were made:— "1749. For removing ye garlands to make ye church lighter ... 1s. 6d."

The garlands were usually shaped like bells or bird-cages, and were constructed on a framework of flexible strips of peeled willow ornamented with ribbons, rosettes and streamers of white materials. Suspended from the inside were gloves, collars and handkerchiefs which had belonged to the deceased, or sometimes with hour-glasses and even egg shells inscribed with an epitaph or appropriate rhyme. The garlands varied in size and value according to the circumstances of the relatives and friends of the deceased. One girl at Glossop was so popular with her acquaintances that they spent the phenomenal sum of £30 on the provision of her funeral garland, and this was more than a century ago!

The garland was carried at the funeral by companions of the deceased girl, and in some instances they wore white calico or muslin hoods tied with black ribbons, and carried long wands of ash or larch. Upon reaching the church porch they formed in parallel lines facing each other and crossed their wands to form an archway beneath which the coffin was carried into church. Some carried baskets of flowers and herbs which they scattered in front of the bier as it proceeded from the lych-gate to the church door and these were the "maiden strewments" of which we shall read a little later. After the service of commital, the garland was hung above the pew which the dead girl had formerly occupied.

Anna Seward, the "Swan of Lichfield", was born at Eyam Rectory and upon removing to Lichfield was in the habit of making an annual pilgrimage to her native village, upon which occasions she was often inspired to write a nostalgic poem. In one of these commemorative poems composed in 1792 she mentions the garlands hanging in Eyam church and draws attention to the fact that young men also qualified for the honour:

Now the low beams with paper garlands hung,
In memory of some village youth or maid,
Draw the soft tear, from thrill'd remembrance sprung;
How oft my childhood marked the tribute paid!
The gloves suspended by the garland's side,
White as its snowy flowers with ribbands tied,
Dear Village! long these wreaths funereal spread,
Simple memorials of thy early dead.

But, as in other villages, the poetical request was ignored and William Wood wrote in 1860:— "No garlands now remain in Eyam Church. It was re-pewed some 30 years ago, and several faded garlands were taken down and destroyed then. I can remember some five or six hanging on nails in the centre of the north aisle, but none have been seen since the time afore-mentioned. The last garland seen at Eyam was carried before the corpse of a Miss Alice Heathcote, a young woman under twenty; it is a little above twenty years ago. The garland and two baskets of flowers, in this instance, were thrown in the grave on the coffin; or rather most of the flowers were strewn between the church gates and church door, and the remainder with the garland thrown into the grave."

The custom is mentioned by Shakespeare in *Hamlet*, when the priest says of Ophelia:

Her obsequies have been so far enlarg'd
As we have warrantise. Her death was doubtful;
And, but for that great command o'ersways the order,
She should in ground unsanctified have lodg'd
Till the last trumpet; for charitable prayers,
Shards, flints, and pebbles, should be thrown on her;
Yet here she is allow'd her virgin crants,
Her maiden strewments, and the bringing home
Of bell and burial.

Why did the priest raise objections to the virgin crants, or garlands, at the funeral of Ophelia? Because of the suspicion attaching to the cause of her death, and the disgrace which was formerly associated with suicide. In those less enlightened days, people who found the burden of life too heavy were vilified by law, authority, and even religion, and were denied burial in "consecrated" ground. The opening of the first scene of the fifth act of the play is introduced with an argument between the sexton clowns concerning the coroner's verdict which had cleared the memory of Ophelia, at least in the eyes of the law, from the shadow of suspicion of suicide.

The custom is of ancient origin, and some authorities claim

that it is descended from the practice of the early Christians who placed floral crowns at the head of deceased virgins. The author of a work entitled the *Comical Pilgrim's Pilgrimage*, published in 1723, wrote: "When a virgin dies, a garland of all sorts of flowers and sweet herbs is carried by a young woman on her head, before the coffin, from which hang down two black ribbons, signifying our mortal state, and two white, as an emblem of purity and innocence. The ends thereof are held by four young maids before whom a basket full of herbs and flowers is supported by two other maids, who strew them along the streets to the place of burial."

William Howitt, the poet, referring to garlands at Heanor, says: "Though I never saw a funeral in which so beautiful and appropriate a practice was retained, I well recollect seeing those gloves and garlands hanging in the church of my native village in Derbyshire, and I have heard my mother say that in her younger days she had helped to cut and prepare them for the funeral of the young women of the place. The garlands were originally of actual flowers—lilies and roses—and the gloves of white kid. For these had been substituted simple white paper. There was a garland then of imitative roses and lilies, wreathed round a bow of peeled willow—a pair of gloves cut in paper, and a white handkerchief of the same material, on which were written some texts of Scripture, or some stanzas of poetry applicable to the occasion and to the hope of immortality of the deceased, and these are not infrequently chosen for the purpose by the dying maiden herself. These emblems of purity and evanescant youth were laid on the coffin during the funeral procession, as the sword and cap of the soldier on his, and were then suspended in the body of the church, and there hung till they fell through time, or till all who had an interest in the deceased were dead or departed."

Such garlands are mentioned as having hung in many Derbyshire churches, including Hope, Eyam, Hathersage, Fairfield, Tissington, Ashover, Bolsover, West Hallam and Crich, where a writer mentions them hanging from the pillars. The only places where they now remain are Matlock, Ashford-in-the-Water and Trusley, where one is preserved beneath a glass case. The Ashford garlands were cleaned and restored at Chatsworth and the Trusley example by experts at the Victoria and Albert Museum, London. When in Matlock or Ashford, I often make a point of calling at the respective churches to see the paper garlands stained and shrivelled with age. Arthur Mee wrote of the Matlock examples: "The most engaging small possession of the church is hanging on the wall of an aisle, a set of six paper garlands. Trifling to those who do not understand, they have a pathetic appeal, for these are funeral garlands, and were carried in the funeral processions of girls who died too soon to marry."

If I worshipped at one of these churches, and the sermon proved too great a tax on my powers of concentration, I fear that my attention would be tempted to stray from the pulpit to the days and plays of Shakespeare. I would half expect to hear the haunting strains of some such melody as "Greensleeves" played by ghostly fingers on a ghostly virginal. And through the misty mirror of memory I would visualise the drifting body of Ophelia so vividly portrayed by Sir John Millais in his painting in the Tate Gallery.

One of the earliest Ashford garlands is dated 12th April, 1747, and was dedicated to the memory of Ann Howard who died at the age of twenty-one. The six lines of poetry have become illegible owing to the fading of the ink. Another bears the inscription:

> Be always ready, no time delay,
> I in my youth was called away;
> Great grief to those that's left behind,
> But I hope I've great joy to find.
> Ann Swindell,
> Aged 22 years,
> Dec. 9th, 1798.

The last garland made at Ashford was for a girl named Blackwell whose tragic death was rather reminiscent of that of Ophelia, for she was drowned in a whirlpool in the River Wye. Another garland in the village of West Hallam bore the tender words:

> For violets which the sweetest showers
> Can ne'er bring back again.

This custom, with its deep emotional appeal, seems to have often inspired contemporary poets, and William Sampson, an early Derbyshire poet whose works are now virtually forgotten, makes a touching allusion to these former funeral rites in a poem dedicated to a Miss E. Tevery who died in 1636. The style and language of the poem may need a little patience and some perseverance in its perusal, but helps to illustrate the antiquity of the ceremonies attaching to the custom:

> Why did the Lilly, Paunce and Violet weepe,
> The Marigold ere sun-set in did creepe?
> At whose reflexion she us'd for to rise
> And at his way-gate to close up here eies.
> Why were the beaten waies with flowers strowne,

41

And set with needy Lazars hanging downe
Their mournful heades? Why did the Pulpit mourne,
As if prepared for some Funerall urne?
Of sweet smelling Flowers, which might belong
Unto some bridall! noe! heaven knowes the cause,
'Twas otherwise decreed in Nature's Lawes;
Those smelling sweetes with which our sense was fed,
Were for the buriall of a maiden, dead.
Which made an Autumme just in the mid-spring,
And all things contrary their births to bring,
Herbs, Plants, and Flowers, contrariously grew
Because they now received not nature's dew,
The needy beggars hung their heades for thee,
Thou matchless map of maiden modesty.
From whose fair hands they had an almner's pay,
As often as they met thee every day . . .
The Maiden Vestalls, that with wat'ry eies,
Before thee to the Church for Vesta's sacrifice,
Were all in white! carracts of innocence
Prefiguring thy greater eminence
So great their losse, that with watery eine,
They offer teares still to thy virgin shrine . . .

The custom was continued in remote parts of Wales until comparatively recent times. The garlands and gloves hung in church for twelve months and were then taken down, and on the actual anniversary of the girl's death her grave was dressed with flowers by her former friends, who also laid a new pair of gloves upon it.

The two garlands obtained by Thomas Bateman from Matlock Church at its restoration over a century ago are illustrated by Llewellynn Jewitt in his first volume of *The Reliquary*, and he describes the larger specimen as follows: — "The hoops and bands **are** decorated with paper flowers, or rosettes, intermixed with bunches of narrow slips, or shreds, of paper; and at the top is a bunch of the same, over paper folded like a fan. Originally, the flowers have been formed, some of plain, others of folded or crimped paper; and others again of both; and in some parts the paper has been afterwards coloured red or blue, thus producing a somewhat gay appearance. From the centre of the top are suspended a pair of gloves, cut out of white paper, with a kerchief or collar, also of paper, gimped on the edges and carefully folded. The hand of the gloves hang below the lower loop."

The custom has often been described as "charming", although this seems to me to be the wrong adjective to use in such a sad ritual and one which must have provoked the most sensitive and tender emotions. For the rustic character has always been a strange blend of sympathy, sentiment and superstition. Yet, on the other hand, such a practice may have had some consolatory value in helping to reconcile both the dying person and her family with the pathos and tragedy of early death. For behind the simple pageantry lurked the sinister shadow of such diseases as tuberculosis, the incidence of which exacted so heavy a toll on young life.

The rule of chastity does not appear to have been rigorously enforced, for the privilege was sometimes extended to young widows who had "enjoyed but one husband". One outstanding exception to the rule was the case of Ann Kendall whose garland hung for many years in the church of South Wingfield, two vicars stoutly resisting offers from prospective purchasers and another finally giving instructions that it should be removed from the church and destroyed! Thus perished another of these sentimental relics. The circumstances attaching to this particular garland were most unusual, for it was carried at the funeral of an unmarried mother. The story of Ann Kendall's misfortune is quite pathetic and excited local sympathy to the extent that she was "allowed her virgin crants" to use the language of Shakespeare. Ann was the attractive daughter of Peter and Mary Kendall who kept the Peacock Inn at Oakerthorpe. She was the belle of the village and local youths vied for her friendship and favour. One of them, a farmer's son, was successful against all rivals and pursued a courtship which the unsuspecting Ann naturally assumed would mature into marriage. But she was seduced by her worthless lover who, even after the birth of her baby daughter, refused to accept the obligations of parenthood. Deceived and distressed, the poor girl was so grieved by his callous indifference that she pined away and died on 14th May, 1745, of what was diagnosed in the village as a broken heart. And that is why, in the words of the poet, Gay,

> *To her sweet memory flowery garlands strung*
> *On her now empty pew aloft were hung.*

But this was not the end of the story. Local indignation could not conceive that such treachery would pass without payment of some penalty, and the day of retribution came soon after Ann's funeral. The youth was riding past the church one day when, suddenly, the bell tolled and his spirited horse took fright, rearing and plunging and flinging its rider to the ground where he was found to be dead.

8. The Wakes

"HUNTING, bull and bear baiting, were the favourite sports of the ancient inhabitants of Hayfield, but on the introduction of commerce they earned high wages, and, indulging in luxury, became effeminate, and their rude sports began to decline ..."

Whether this old writer would have included dancing under the category of "rude" sports, we shall never know, but students of folk music will always be indebted to Hayfield for Derbyshire's most famous folk-song inspired by the fairs formerly held in this township. I say "township" because Hayfield would appear to have had higher civic status than a village in that it once boasted a mayor. As recently as 1844, a grand dinner was held to mark the inauguration of Mr. Joseph Bowden to this office, and we read that his predecessor, Mr. John Hobson, had occupied the position for thirty years. It would be interesting to know whether the dignitaries who held this appointment wore a mayoral chain or other insignia of office.

In his *Tour through the Peak of Derbyshire* (1809), Hutchinson describes a visit to Hayfield Fair upon which he purchased an original copy of the well-known song. The text has been modified with passing years to make it more intelligible and the metre a little less flexible. But here is what Hutchinson wrote:—
"Having arrived at Hayfield, I found it was the fair day. This had enticed the country lads and lasses, though nearly up to the knees in dirt. No enjoyment could be found here, but that of taking possession of a corner in a large room, and smoking the observing pipe. In one part of it there was a country man, in a smock frock, attempting to dance a hornpipe, to the great entertainment of his friends and neighbours around him. In another, a comical genius was singing a song with particular glee; one of which I immediately bought, and have transcribed a copy, which will serve the reader as some description of

The Humours of Hayfield Fair

Come, lasses and lads, take leave of your dads,
  And, away to the fair let's hie;
For every lad has gotten his lass,
  And a fiddler standing by;

For, Jenny has gotten her Jack,
  And Nancy had gotten her Joe
With Dolly and Tom, good lack,
  How they jig it to and fro.

Ritum, raddleum, raddleum—ritum, raddleum, ri;
Ritum, raddleum, raddleum—ritum, raddleum, ri.

My heart 'gain ribs ga' thumps,
  When I went to th' wake or fair,
Wi' a pair of new sol'd pumps,
  To dance when I got there;
I'd ride grey nag I swore,
  And were mounted like a king,
Cousin Dickey walk'd on a'fore,
  Driving a pig tied wi' a string.

        Ritum, raddleum, etc.

Pally Simpson, too, was there,
  "Wi' 'Neighbour how do you do?'
There were all the world at the fair,
  And drunk 'till they were fou',
'Twas neither heigh! nor gee!
  For soon as I sold my cow,
The fiddler shog'd his knee,
  And I danced my pumps clean through.

        Ritum, raddleum, etc.

You're out, says Dick—I'm not, says Nick,
  The fiddler plays it false,
And so says Hugh, and so says Sue,
  And so says nimble Al'ce;
The fiddler did agree,
  To right us in a crack,
Dance face to face, says he,
  And then dance back to back.

        Ritum, raddleum, etc.

Thus after an hour they tript to a bower,
  To play for ale and cakes,
And kisses too, until they were due,
  The maidens held the stakes;
The women then began
  To quarrel with the men,

And bad them take their kisses back,
  And gi' 'em their own again!

  Ritum, raddleum, etc.

Thus they sat, until it were late,
  And they tir'd the fiddler quite,
Wi' singing and playing, without any paying,
  From morning until it were night:
They told the fiddler then,
  They'd pay him for his play,
And each gave two-pence,
(Speaking) *(Ey, they gave two-pence a piece)*
  And then they hopp'd away.

  Ritum, raddleum, etc.

Come Dolly, says I, now homeward hie,
  And I'll go wi' thee a mile,
She twinkled her eyes with a sigh,
  As I handed her over the style;
Then I cuddled and kiss'd her face;
  Were I much to blame?
Had you been in my place,
(Speaking) *(I don't mean you in the smock frock, dancing a*
                                                  hornpipe—
I mean that sly-looking fellow, smoking his pipe in the
                                                  corner,)
  I vow you'd ha' done the same.

  Ritum, raddleum, etc."

Imagination visualises the sprightly Jenny, Nancy, Alice, Dolly
and Sue, with flushed and dimpled cheeks, as they capered nimbly
with their robust partners to the feverish music of the fiddler,
watched enviously by those whose age and arthritis denied the
same privilege, but which complaints could not deny them their
memories of former fair days. We wonder what sort of person-
ality the ingratiating Pally Simpson must have been that she
should have the distinction of being singled out as expressing
concern for the welfare of her neighbours. Or Cousin Dickey with
his pig tethered by a piece of string. And in addition to the
characters mentioned in the song, we would be interested to
know a little more about the uninhibited yokel performing his
doddering dance, dressed in his best smock frock, and his rival,
the comic singer, interpolating his impromptu comments into the
script of the song. Not to mention the reporter of the scene

smoking his contemplative pipe in the corner. What a pity that Hayfield had no contemporary William Hogarth present with pencil and sketchbook to preserve such scenes for the enjoyment of posterity!

And one cannot help wondering whether any of the restless dancing throngs of erstwhile fairs were among the spirits of 1745 who "to the great astonishment and Terror of several spectators deserted the Coffin, and arising out of the grave, immediately ascended directly towards Heaven, singing in Consert all along as they mounted thro' the Air . . ." For the reverend writer to whom we are indebted for the vivid account of this happening at Hayfield, further reported "that they had no winding sheets about them, yet did not appear quite naked, their Vesture seem'd streak'd with gold, interlaced with sable, skirted with white, yet thought to be exceeding light by the agility of their motions, and the swiftness of their ascent. They left a most fragrant and delicious Odour behind them, but were quickly out of sight, and what is become of them or in what distant Regions of this vast System they have since fixed their Residence, no Mortal can tell." Perhaps they are tapping their feet to the rhythm of some dance in a heavenly Hayfield Fair.

Robert Murray Gilchrist wrote: — "To-day the Peaklanders are as fond of dancing as ever, and although no piper produces eerie music at feast times they can still make a pretty show. The hill country has endowed the youths and maidens with suppleness and they trip it with exceeding grace. . . . Old customs are tenaciously preserved—in some places the wells are dressed with flowers for the festival of the patron saint, and in one of the most remote villages every Royal Oak Day a quaint and pretty pageant enlivens the irregular grey streets. At such times the kin from far-distant towns return to the old home and spend a few hours of merry-making." The 17th century historian, Philip Kinder, reported: "In the Peak they are much given to dance after the baggpipes, almost every town hath a baggpipe in it." During the Highlanders retreat in 1745, a piper strayed into the village of Eyam and was kept occupied all night playing his "bellows" in one of the inns.

An alternative and more popular name for the Fair is that mentioned in the Hayfield song as the Wake; a word which is often pluralised by misuse and misunderstanding. The Wake has gradually changed from a sacred to a secular festival, having passed through various phases which reflect steadily changing social trends, until it assumed a pattern which has little relevance to the patronal festival it was designed to commemorate. As the name suggests, it was a wake or vigil in which clergy, choir and congregation observed a watch-night service to welcome the particular saint's day to which their church was dedicated. The following day was devoted to Maypole and Morris dancing, cock-fighting, bull- and bear-baiting, wrestling and pugilism.

Then came the pedlars and hucksters displaying their gaudy wares to tempt the purses and the pockets of the rustic population. They were followed by amusement caterers with coconut shies, swing-boats, helter-skelters, shooting galleries, boxing booths and stalls for the sale of gingerbread and striped humbugs, with perhaps the closely curtained tent of a gipsy fortune-teller. At night-time the fairground was lit by paraffin flares which spilled a flickering light on the eager upturned faces of children and adults, creating scenes which would have captivated the imagination and engaged the pencil or brush of artists like Joseph Wright of Derby. And, later still, came the mechanical amusements—roundabouts, cake-walks, dodgems and chair-o-planes. Traction engines generated electricity to supply power to operate the new and more exciting forms of entertainment and to feed galaxies of coloured bulbs which, in themselves, were a novelty to people whose homes were lit by paraffin or gas. The fiddle and pipe paled into insignificance against the powerful music of organs which digested perforated sheets of music as brightly painted figures beat drums and clashed cymbals to the wonder of the onlooker, while pioneer one-armed bandits picked the unsuspecting pockets of those who visualised a cascade of coins being generously returned for their investment of a few coppers.

One of the earlier Wakes-time scenes was described by Dr. S. T. Hall, after paying a visit to Eyam nearly two centuries ago. "My last visit chanced to be about the middle of the 'wakes week'; and while passing along the street, the pipe and fiddle would occasionally greet my ear with their merry notes from one of the little inns with which the village abounds; and a game of cricket was coming off in a nearby field around which many of the inhabitants had gathered as spectators. With these exceptions, and that of a few stalls for the sale of knicknacks and sweetmeats, on which groups of chubby children were casting their longing looks, there was no external signs of a carnival exhibited."

Another incidental reference to this annual event at Eyam claimed notice in the *Gentleman's Magazine* and mentions the custom of Morris dancing in the village. "At Eyam, August 28, 1802, in the County of Derby, Edward Dooley, Miner and Musician. An Oratorio had been intended to be performed at Eyam Church on the following Sunday (the wakes) for his benefit, as he was very poor and infirm. Too much anxiety and exertion in preparing for the occasion hastened his end, which unexpectedly took place the evening before the intended performance. Being in company with some young men, who were rehearsing a

Morris dance, which was to be held the following Monday in Eyam Edge, a mountain top near Eyam, he suddenly laid down his fiddle and expired. The Oratorio was performed the next day for the benefit of his mother, an aged widow, with whom he had lived." Dooley's fiddle was preserved in the village for many years.

In 1785 a Base Voile (bassoon) was acquired for Youlgreave Church, and a vestry meeting directed that the instrument should be used solely for worship, and was "not to be handled about the Wakes or any other place of profaneness and Diversion." Exception was made, however, for the club feasts of Youlgreave, Winster and Elton. When friendly societies were at the height of their popularity, members adopted the Wakes for their annual club feasts when officials wore their regalia and the lodge banners were carried in procession.

J. B. Firth (*Highways and Byways of Derbyshire*) tells of a communal dance at Eyam which appears to be rather similar to the Helston Floral Dance, when residents at the top of the village danced into their neighbour's house like the Pied Piper to conscript the occupants, then to the next house, and so through the length of the village until the houses were empty and the street full of dancing people.

The Wakes was a time for family reunion. The boy who was indentured to a tradesman or farmer, and the daughter employed in domestic service, returned for a few days' holiday. Stephen Glover says: — "The village wakes or feasts are very prevalent seasons of festivity and amusement throughout this county. They begin on Sunday, and continue through most, or perhaps all, of the ensuing week. Mr. Farey says that these rural festivals were thought by many well-informed persons with whom he conversed, to be rather beneficial than otherwise. A thorough cleaning of the cottage, and mostly a white-washing of its rooms, annually precedes the wakes; the children and parents are then, if possible, new clothed." In some instances the churches were spring-cleaned for the occasion, as we have recorded in Hayfield Churchwardens' Accounts: — "1766. Paid for cleaning the Chapel at the Wakes ... 1s. 0d."

Another feature of the Wakes in former days was the baking of a special confection called "wakes cakes". These delicacies were as much a part of the Wakes as mince-pies and plum puddings were of Christmas. This traditional confection is referred to in the Hayfield Fair ballad where "after an hour they went to a bower and played for ales and cakes." They also figure again—in conjunction with the ever popular beverage, ale—in a jingle concerning villages near Matlock: —

Winster Wakes there's ale and cakes,
Elton Wakes there's quenchers;
Bircher Wakes there's knives and forks,
Wensley Wakes there's wenches.

When the Derbyshire Federation of Women's Institutes compiled a county cookery book, several villages volunteered recipes for their traditional wakes cakes—Winster, Wirksworth, Ashbourne, Kirk Langley and others. Some readers may be interested in a specimen of such dainties, and here is the recipe from Winster. The ingredients are: ½lb. plain flour; one egg; 6 ozs. butter; one ounce currants and 6 ozs. castor sugar, and the method: Rub flour and butter together, add sugar and currants, mix to a stiff dough with the beaten egg. knead a little, roll out and bake in a moderate oven. The cakes should be a pale golden brown and the size of a saucer.

Winster has not only preserved the formula for its wakes cakes, but it has had the foresight to retain its five traditional dances—the Winster Reel, Gallop, Processional, Morris and Butterfly. The doggerel rhyme which helped the dancers to remember their steps has also been preserved. It closely resembles the rhyme which the dancers used to hum at Castleton Garland Ceremony, so much so that one suspects there may be some infringement of copyright. It runs:

This is it and that is it,
And this is a Morris dancer,
A piper fell and broke his neck
And said it was a chancer;
Oh! you dunno an' I dunno
What fun we had at Brampton,
A roasted pig, a cuddle duck,
An' a puddin' baked i' a lantern.

Other villages have evolved their own country dance patterns and the Tideswell Processional Morris was recorded by Sharp and MacIlwaine in 1912 and published by Novello and Company. It was reported at the time that "the Processional Morris is danced annually at Tideswell by the members of the Oddfellows' Club, at 6-30 p.m. on the Monday in Wakes Week, i.e. the week following the Sunday nearest to June 24th. The procession, which this year consisted of about twenty-four couples, is headed by the band. The dancers are dressed in their ordinary clothes, without coats, and wear the regalia of their Order. The procession starts from the Club House, and passes along the main streets of the town, drawing up before the chief houses, inns, etc. Before each of these the dance is performed in a stationary position for a few minutes, after which a short pause is made, the dancers partake of refreshment, and pass on. On the following Thursday, School-feast Day, the dance is performed by the school-children and adults of both sexes; and again on the Saturday by the junior members of the Oddfellows' Club."

Kit-dressing, a custom usually associated with May Day, was carried out during the Wakes at Baslow as recorded by Stephen Glover: — "At Baslow, the rural festival of kit-dressing took place on the 4th of August, and in the present year (1829) the procession was attended by the Baslow Band, and the decoration of the kits (wooden milk pails) surpassed in beauty and taste any that have ever before been seen. There were a great number of persons from the surrounding country, and even more distant places, assembled to witness this rural fete, which gave unusual delight. On one of the kits was this inscription: —

> *The farmer, the plough-boy, the fleece, and the flail,*
> *Success to the milk-maid who carries the pail.*

"A beautiful garland and a large pink-coloured flag with emblems, were also carried in the procession. Twigs of willow were bent over the tops of the kits, and entwined with ribbons and flowers; and many fanciful ornaments of muslin and silk, mingled with trinkets of silver and gold composed the garlands, which were also formed upon a frame-work of willow twigs, interwoven together. The maidens of the village, attired in their best, carried the kits on their heads, attended by the young men. In the evening a happy company assembled at the Wheat Sheaf Inn, where dancing and merriment concluded the day's festivities."

Although we may regret the passing of such appealing customs, we rejoice that the more barbarous "sports" of baiting animals and cock-fighting have also either died away or been suppressed by law. Quite a few villages have preserved their bull-rings. At Bonsall, one is preserved in the church still attached to the boulder by which it was anchored to the ground. Another is to be seen at the foot of the village cross on the green at Foolow, while at Eyam and Snitterton the rings are preserved "in situ" and protected by iron covers. At Chesterfield a byelaw existed whereby butchers bringing bulls to be slaughtered at The Shambles were compelled to bait the animals, or pay a fine of 3s. 4d. It was believed that baiting made the beef more tender.

Cock-fighting was carried on at many public-houses and there is a ballad entitled "The Hathersage Cocking". One verse runs: —

> *Then great Bill Brown came swagg'ring down,*
> *I'll hold you a guinea to a crown,*

That let the black Cock have fair play,
And he'll drive the sod of the Bonny Gray,

Singing tol de rol de riddle lol de ray,
Tol lol de riddle lol de ray.

Between the two world wars, as people grew more prosperous, and factories, mills, mines and quarries were closed for a week (then a fortnight with pay!), the operatives and their families were able to afford a holiday at the coast or even abroad. Villages became deserted and dead for the annual Wakes and the amusement caterers found it no longer profitable to pitch their caravans for a whole week. Well-dressings were revived and carnivals became increasingly popular so that in many villages the Wake again begins with a religious service and ends with a secular rejoicing; again it begins at the altar—e'en though it be one of flowers—and ends at the bar of the public-house.

The Derby Morris dance team at Castleton (Sheffield Morning Telegraph).

The 1961 well-dressing at Eyam.

The well-dressing designed by the author to commemorate the 300th anniversary of the plague at Eyam.

Well-dressers engaged in "petalling" at Wormhill.

A Christmas posset pot (both photos: Davy and United Engineering Co. Ltd.).

A striking print of Derbyshire carol singers, including Samuel Slack of Tideswell and Chadwick of Hayfield.

9.   A Well-Dressing at Wormhill

"JUST before the shady Dale is contracted between the precipices, the bubbling brook from Wormhill dashes down from ledge to ledge of its sequestered dell, in noisy tumult, beneath the overhanging verdure. Where the streamlet bursts from its earth-bound course, the ancient custom of well-dressing was kept up, as at Tissington, within living memory, and the peasantry of the neighbourhood used to awake the echoes of the ravine with the sounds of their rustic jollity."

This paragraph was written by John Leyland in his book, *The Peak of Derbyshire*, which was published in 1891, and it was just sixty years later that the custom was revived in Wormhill as a Festival of Britain celebration. The experiment proved so successful and rewarding to the villagers that they decided to make well-dressing an annual occasion, and ever since the village has been a shrine of pilgrimage to admirers of this ancient art.

The site chosen for the occasion was the Brindley Well in the centre of the village, and ever since the screen has been erected at this site, nor can we imagine a more suitable setting. The people of Wormhill have been fortunate in securing the help and advice of Mr. Oliver Shimwell, of Tideswell, who is the ace of well-dressing designers in Derbyshire. His work has a distinction and a difference which makes it outstanding in quality, and he has achieved a measure of perfection and finesse which has yet to be equalled, let alone excelled, in the county, for a lifetime's experience of choosing and using material in this novel media goes into the interpretation of every design he undertakes. A native of Youlgreave, where his father was prominent in the exercise of well-dressing, Mr. Shimwell has been a missionary of the media, introducing it to Stoney Middleton and Tideswell as well as Wormhill.

In 1953 Mr. Shimwell had the distinction of presenting the first well-dressing to the citizens of London when the Tideswell team created a picture of Westminster Abbey which was erected in the Dean's Yard to reinforce an appeal for funds to restore this national shrine. At a later date Mr. Shimwell designed a picture of St. Paul's Cathedral and this stood proudly on the steps of the great church to encourage an appeal for funds to aid its restoration from war damage. Sir Christopher Wren must never have imagined a portrait of his grand architectural design would be reproduced in flower petals, seeds, mosses and other natural materials!

Now well-dressing is admittedly a purely rustic art, yet it provides the artist with a challenging medium. He creates his collage of colour with living materials; not with crushed pigments of paint, the spun fibre of wool, nor yet with cold, inanimate stone. He uses the velvet of freshly plucked petals, mosses and lichens peeled from stone walls, larch and alder cones, seed-pods, leaves, ferns, and other vegetable matter.

The floral artist never despises any material in his quest for exact colouring, or to achieve the right visual effect. Dead laurel leaves have been used to simulate the mellowed wood of a violin; decayed ivy leaves piped with nettle stems to reproduce an ancient door shadowed with masonry of grey lichen; lupin pods have provided the grey for leaden fall-pipes. Angels with feathers of marguerite petals, have swept the strings of harps of calendula gold, and ladies have been graced with charming crinoline gowns of pink or blue hydrangea. Strips of bark and hemlock seeds tipped with geranium buds have produced an artist's brush threaded through a palette of leaves splashed with daubs of colour suggested by petals of various hues. Golden oat straws have been used for the gilt edges of an open book, while rushes were used to reproduce the shading of the opposite edges.

Petals are used for the lighter colouring effects, blending into a wonderful concentration of colour, and suggesting to the onlooker something of the luminous appearance of stained glass. Years of experience determine which materials last the longest, for some petals are so frail that they will soon wilt and shrivel, or lose their freshness in a few days. Quite often the artist has to make last minute improvisations, for, in the event of a dry summer, flowers can be so advanced that, although normally plentiful at a certain season, they may no longer be in bloom or may be in very short supply. The opposite effect may obtain in the event of a wet summer. Those who take part in well-dressing know full well that it has its problems and pains as well as its pleasures. It taxes the patience of the workers as much as their resourcefulness, and the custom was made the theme of a comedy, *Bless the Well*, written by Dr. L. du Garde Peach, the Derbyshire playwright, and produced in 1958 by the now defunct Great Hucklow Players in their Village Theatre.

The actual origin of this ancient custom is unknown. Some writers believe it to be a possible survival of the Roman festival of Fontinalus which may have been introduced into Britain by the occupation forces and lingered on after their return to Rome.

One can imagine how this custom must have appealed to the craftsmen who created such wonderful mosaic floors from coloured cubes of stone for the villas of their wealthy patrons. Water was much esteemed by the Romans. The divination of water, particularly any charged with health-restoring minerals or salts, seems to have been instinct in this highly civilised race. Wherever they went, they located springs which possessed curative properties, applying the water to medical needs as well as to those of drinking and domestic sanitation. They may have lacked an analytical understanding of the chemical composition of water, but they did not lack appreciation of its benefits, and dedicated the springs in honour of water nymphs and deities to whom they ascribed the healing virtue. Some trace the custom to the pagan worship of spirits believed to have inhabited springs and streams, when flowers were scattered upon the surface of the water as votive offerings. It is known that efforts were made by the primitive Church to suppress this form of indigenous ritual, but although it was condemned by the Synod of Arles in 452, and forbidden in the canons of St. Anselm in 1102, it still persisted in a Christianised form as a thanksgiving for water with its threefold values of cleansing, healing and refreshing. Finding that they could not wean their converts from the idea of water worship, the early missionaries appear to have compromised and re-dedicated the springs to saints of the early Church.

The custom of garlanding wells with chaplets of flowers was once prevalent all over the country, particularly those which were believed to have healing value, but the development of well-flowering in its present form can be traced to Tissington where the ceremony has been observed on Ascension Day for several centuries. There are two rival traditions as to how the custom began, and both may be true in parts. One claims that, at the beginning of the 17th century there was an epidemic of plague from which the people of Tissington escaped and, believing their immunity to be due to the purity of their water, they started the festival as an act of gratitude to God. The other story attributes the origin of the custom to the same period when the county was parched by drought and, because the springs never failed, they were festooned with flowers as a thanksgiving. Parish records confirm that Derbyshire suffered from both disease and drought at this period.

In Youlgreave parish register is the record:— "1615. A Dry Summer. There was no rayne fell uppon the earth from the 25th day of March until the 2nd day of May, and there was but one shower; after which there fell none tyll the 18th day of June, and then there fell another; after y[t] there fell none at all tyll the 4th day of August, after which tyme there was sufficient rayne upon the earth; so that the greatest p^t of this land, specially the south p^{ts} were burnt upp, both corne and hay. An ordinary Sumer load of hay was 2li, and little or none to be got for money. This p^t of the peake was very sore burnt upp, only Lankishyre and Cheshyre had rayne ynough all the Sumer; and both corne and hay sufficient."

Originally, well-dressing was celebrated in simple and inartistic fashion by hanging chaplets and garlands of flowers over the wells. Then geometrical patterns were introduced, often incorporating a vase, cascade or fountain in the design. Eventually the portrayal of Biblical and architectural scenes became popular and this continues in general practice today. The subject of water—Moses striking the rock, Elijah pouring his libation over the sacrificial altar on Mount Carmel, the Woman at the well of Sychar—was usually included in the design. But artists have subsequently widened the scope in much more imaginative ways, and in one village the style of Mabel Lucy Atwell has been successfully copied in this media.

The method employed in constructing these floral mosaics has also developed into quite a complicated process, with elaborate wooden screens providing the foundations for the display. Active preparations begin several days before the actual ceremonies, although the designs are often drawn months before. Clay, which has been soaking in large baths, has to be "puddled" by hand to extract pieces of stone and grit, and then squeezed through the fingers and kneaded to a smooth creamy consistency before being trowelled on to the screens which are like huge, shallow wooden trays pierced with holes and studded with nails to help key the clay in position.

Lengths of lining paper, or paper table cloths, on which the designs have been drawn, are then laid on the surface of the clay so that the lines can be traced through with a tailor's pricking-wheel, cocktail sticks, skewers, shoemaker's awls or any other sharp instrument. After the paper has been carefully peeled off, the outlines of the impressions left on the clay are piped with maize, rice, beans, larch or alder cones and hemlock seeds, following which lichens, leaves, mosses, seeds and other durable materials are pressed into place. The flower petals (deliberately left until the last to prevent them being stained with clay, and because of their fragility) are then inserted and laid overlapping each other like the scales of a fish or the tiles on a roof. According to the strict canons of well-dressing tradition, all the materials must have grown in fields, gardens, hedgerows and woods, while fluorspar, calcite and other minerals or manufactured materials are regarded—although used in some villages—as a violation of the art. The tools of the well-dressing team are often quite simple and improvised from skewers, tweezers, hairgrips, matchsticks and scissors. The scissors are useful for shaping and trimming, while the tweezers come in handy for the delicate work of removing unsatisfactory material. ...

It was the Friday evening before August Bank Holiday when I called to see the Wormhill workers putting the finishing touches to their screen. The scene of activity was one of the most spacious barns I have seen, and I imagined that it must have been comparable in size to the nave of nearby Tideswell Church. The building had no windows, except in the roof, and these illumined the films of spider webs which ornamented the supporting roof timbers as the evening light filtered into the interior. The sides were lined with agricultural implements and machinery; wagons, drays, tractors and even cars, while the centre was occupied by sections of the screens resting on bales of straw. The surrounding floor was strewn with a debris of torn petals, soiled leaves, spilled beans and berries, and the broken stems from which flower petals had been shredded. Nearby stood a cluster of jars and pails containing surplus blooms of hydrangea, zinnia, marguerites and other flowers.

The petalling team worked on quietly, but intently, patiently building up the mosaic of cones, lichens, mosses and petals, carefully selecting each flake of colour and inserting it into the clay with a skill and experience gained over many years. There was an atmosphere of concentration, almost of tension, as the work grew beneath their fingers. Occasionally a worker would pause to confer with Mr. Shimwell on the choice or use of some material, then deftly snip a leaf or petal to the exact shape before pressing it lightly into position. Sometimes they retired a short distance to survey the effect of their work, or bent over the picture to snatch or blow away some surplus material.

As the concentration of colour continued to evolve beneath the painstaking fingers of the workers, it gradually took shape and semblance to the small copy which provided a blue-print to the correct shades and hues, and I thought of the progress made in the composition of such scenes since R. Murray Gilchrist described the uncouth results of a well-dressing a century ago. He describes the floral tableau in his novel, *Willowbrake*, published in 1898, although the crudeness of effect is probably exaggerated: — "Two lumbering conveyances drew up in front of the well. A crowd gathered to watch the proceedings. Bagshawe and Palfreyman disappeared behind the curtain and exhibited their handiwork. Both scenes were grotesquely ugly. The old cobbler had no knowledge of outline, and the Sower would have filled with dread any of the monstrous gargoyles of the church, whilst the basket from which he flung handfuls of clodlike seeds resembled more than ought else a battered coalscuttle. The Ploughman was even more grotesque—a caricature

61

which might easily have been confounded with a child's attempt
to depict Samson swinging the ass's jawbone ..."

But he continues with the description of a more attractive
effort produced by a more artistic designer:— "It was in truth a
pretty thing—so pretty, indeed, that the beholders regretted its
perishableness. The Reaper, a woman in a long white gown,
made lacelike by the loose meadowsweet, held a sickle of glisten-
ing silverweed that curved about an armful of wheat. The face
and hands and feet were formed of pink and white thrift, the eyes
were of blue periwinkle, the lips of rose petals, and the hair of
finely interwoven yellow bracken ..."

Joseph Hatton, in *The Dagger and the Cross*, describes a well-
dressing in Eyam which purports to have taken place just before
the outbreak of plague. Much as we would like to think the
incident was based upon fact, we fear that the account was
transferred from Tissington for the sake of literary convenience,
although this does not preclude such a happening in Eyam at
that time for the custom had by then spread to other places since
its revival at the former village early in the 17th century. Hatton
writes:— "But in a general way, the original well-decorators of
Derbyshire were villagers, who, with the same instinct that one
sees in even the most primitive people, contrived pieces of orna-
mental design of singular grace, and with the impulse of worship.
There was a hearty rivalry among the village artists in their
schemes of decoration, but they all had a similar method. In the
first place a wooden frame of the shrine to be erected was made;
it was constructed in parts; so that it was portable and easy of
treatment. Each section was covered with clay, mixed with salt
to preserve its moisture. Upon the clay the native artist drew
the pattern he intended to fill, and this he embroidered with
flowers. The buds and blossoms, twigs, leaves and grasses were
pressed into the design and manipulated with a tool, the result
being a kind of mosaic, as rich as tapestry. Sometimes the designs
were realisations of an existing work of art, but they were mostly
fantastic efforts at ornamentation, embodying a text or a symbol,
the effect being often both beautiful and impressive." Hatton's
novel was published in 1897. ...

Eventually the Wormhill picture was complete and the sections
of glowing colour were tenderly lifted upon three drays drawn by
tractors. These set off in slow procession—I was reminded of the
solemnity of a funeral procession, but the pace was to prevent
jolting of the precious freight—to the site at Brindley's Well
where they were carefully erected under the direction of Mr.
Shimwell. When the last section was finally fitted into position,
the workers stood grouped around discussing the result of their
labour with obvious satisfaction and apparently reluctant to leave
the floral shrine to resume their domestic or farm duties.

The picture was a coronation of colour which arrested and held the attention by its sovereign dignity. The incident illustrated in the central panel was the parable of the Good Samaritan, and all the element of original drama was represented in the scene. The victim of assault, with bandaged limb and torn garments, was supported by the kneeling figure of the sympathetic Samaritan. Their garments were woven from zinnia petals falling in folds of varying colour. Hills of grey and gold lichen were slashed with dark green laurel leaves for shadow, with the same material reversed to supply the lighter slopes. The tips of distant hills were etched against a sky of mottled hydrangea petals, giving them a sinister appearance which fitted the wild and lonely landscape which the imagination conceives would be a suitable setting for the parable.

The caption and title of the subject were worked in bold letters of red geranium against a camomile background, and the pastel blue and white hydrangea petals of the side panels suggested the delicate colouring of Wedgwood. At the foot of these panels were two intricate designs which had been inspired by a tile in the floor of Lichfield Cathedral. Mr. Shimwell confided that he often got ideas for his designs from a visit to a cathedral; perhaps a carved panel of wood or stone; the decoration of a pillar; the pattern of a tile on the floor; a section of mosaic, or a fragment from a stained glass window.

The semi-circular pediment was emblazoned with the arms of the See of Canterbury surmounted by a mitre with supporting decoration worked in zinnias, hydrangeas, buttercups and statice, while on either side corbels and finials bore blue cornflower and red geranium crosses. The central feature of the mantel was the date in geraniums on a background of white hydrangea petals, with a flanking design of mottled statice.

And so the completed picture stood, radiant in its exotic and living beauty, like a gigantic sampler embroidered in brilliant floral stitches, an act of worship wrought by hand and not spoken by lips. Not only an act of worship, but an object of wonder and admiration which the following evening was the focus of a service of thanksgiving for water with its purifying, refreshing, healing, germinating and generating powers, and, remembering James Brindley, a native of the parish, its use as a means of travel and transport. Nor must we overlook its spiritual significance as a symbol of cleansing in the Christian rite of baptism. And all through the following week the village was a shrine of pilgrimage to admirers of this ancient custom which, although once frowned upon by the early Church, has again become one of its festivals of rejoicing and thanksgiving.

The custom was adopted at Wirksworth in 1827 as an expression of appreciation of an early water scheme financed by a group of local benefactors who had water conveyed from the moors through wooden pipes to taps sited in various parts of the town. One former resident, Susan L. Marsden, left a legacy of £100, the interest of which was to be disbursed each year in prizes to encourage children to continue the craft. Youlgreave introduced the scheme two years later to mark the erection by public subscription, of the large stone tank—the Fountain—in the centre of the village. Similar motives prompted the people of Buxton to start the custom in 1840 when the Duke of Devonshire provided their town with a piped supply.

In the same year Barlow commenced dressing wells to mark an improved water supply to the village, although it is claimed that the villagers carried out the custom over three hundred years ago. Whole flowers, including rambler roses, are used in the composition of the floral pictures, and this technique is called "blossoming" as distinct from "petalling". The screens are protected by canvas awnings and they are presented in a triptych style. In recent years, more and more villages have either revived or adopted the custom and well-dressing has become one of Derbyshire's most popular tourist attractions.

The village of Endon in Staffordshire perpetuates a form of well-dressing on the 29th May, and the custom was introduced or revived to commemorate the provision of a piped supply of water to the village. There almost seems to be a relationship with the Castleton Garland ceremony held on the same day, for the well was originally decorated in simple fashion with boughs and flowers, but the technique of petalling used in well-flowering was developed at a later date. Robert Plot (*The Natural History of Staffordshire*, 1686) seems to suggest that it was originally a link with Rogationtide for the custom was carried out at the "gospel places". He wrote:— "they have also a custom in this country ... of adorning their wells with boughs and flowers: this it seems they do at all gospel places whether wells, trees or hills: which being now observed only for decency and custom sake is innocent enough ... it was usual to pay this respect to such wells as were eminent in curing distemper, on the saints day whose name the well bore, diverting themselves with cakes and ale, and a little music and dancing, which, whilst within these bounds was also innocent recreation."

In conclusion, the reader may be interested to know that, in addition to articles, poems, plays and hymns having been inspired in praise of this ancient custom, it has also been made the subject of a musical cantata entitled *The Dressing of the Wells*, the libretto written by A. J. Foxwell and the music by Alfred Moffat. The publishers were J. Curwen and Sons, London, but the work is now out of print.

10. Rushing Bearing and Other Rural Customs

A WRITER in 1528 accused Thomas a Becket of extravagance in the use of rushes as a floor covering, saying that "he was man-full in his household, for his Hall was every daye in somer strewed with green rushes, and in wynter with clene hey, for to save the Knyghtes clothes that sate on the flore for defaute of place to syt on." In 1587, Thomas Newton wrote in his *Herball to the Bible* concerning the "sedge and rushes with which many of the country do use in summer time to strawe their parlors and churches, as well for cooleness as for pleasant smell." For many years, rushes were used to carpet the floors of village churches, and, once each year, these were swept out and substituted with clean, sweet- smelling sheaves of fresh rushes mown in marshy meadows and left to dry in the summer sun. Like many other events in rural life, this renewal of the rushes was made the occasion of religious rejoicing and festivity.

One writer describes the ceremony as follows: — "They cut hard rushes from the marsh, which they make up into long bundles, and then dress them in fine linen, silk ribbons, flowers, &c. Afterwards, the young women in the village, who perform the ceremony that year, take up the burden erect, and begin the procession (precedence being always given to the churchwarden's burden), which is attended with music, drums, &c. Setting down their burdens in the church, they strip them of their ornaments, leaving the heads or crowns of them decked with flowers, cut papers, &c. Then the company return and cheerfully partake of a cold collation, and spend the remaining part of the day and night in dancing round a maypole, adorned with flowers."

Some writers claim that this custom originated from the Druid practice of strewing places consecrated to their deities with rushes. Although it is no longer practised in Derbyshire, the custom persists over the Cheshire border at Macclesfield Forest Church where a hymn was specially written for the occasion. It includes the verses: —

Our fathers these same floors have trod
Whereon these rushes have been laid,
And now within the Realms of God,
From earthly sorrows free are made.

And grant, dear Saviour, in Thy love,
That all who here green tributes gave,
Within Thy temple blest above,
The palm of victory may wave.

References made to rushes and the rush-carts in the church-wardens' accounts of several Derbyshire churches recall the prevalence of the custom in the county. At Ballidon the chapel was annually strewn with rushes until the year 1822. Hay, mown in the Church Meadows, was used at Whitwell, and straw was used at Scarcliffe because of the scarcity of rushes. In the Hayfield Churchwardens' Accounts are the entries: — "1766. Upon the account of the Rush Cart . . . 5s. od." and "1722. For rushes for church . . . 2s. 6d."

Farey, in his *Survey of Derbyshire* published in 1815, wrote: — "An ancient custom still prevails in Chapel-en-le-Frith, Glossop, Hayfield, Mellor, Peak Forest, and other places in the north of the county, I believe, of keeping the floor of the church and pews therein, constantly strewed or littered with dried rushes; the process of renewing which annually is called the Rush-bearing, and is usually accompanied by much ceremony. The Rush-bearing in Peak Forest is held on Midsummer Eve in each year. In Chapel-en-le-Frith, I was informed, that their Rush-bearing usually takes place in the latter end of August, on public notice from the churchwardens, of the rushes being mown and properly dried, in some marshy parts of the parish, where the young people assemble, and having loaded the rushes on carts, decorate the same with flowers and ribbons, and attend them in procession to the church; many of them huzzaing and cracking whips by the side of the rush-carts on their way thither; and where everyone present lends a hand in carrying and spreading the rushes. In Whitwell, instead of rushes, the hay of a piece of grass land called the Church-close, is annually, on Midsummer Eve, carted to and spread in the church."

Ebenezer Rhodes, in his *Peak Scenery* (1822), described the custom at Glossop. "We visited the village church, a plain and lowly structure, and as little ornamented in the interior as it is without. Here we observed the remains of some garlands hung up near the entrance into the chancel. They were mementoes of a custom of rather a singular nature, that lingers about this part of Derbyshire, after having been lost in nearly every other. It is denominated 'Rush-bearing'; and the ceremonies of this truly rural fete take place, annually, on one of the days appointed to the wake or village festival. A car or waggon is on this occasion decorated with rushes. A pyramid of rushes, ornamented with wreaths of flowers, and surmounted with a garland, occupies the centre of the car, which is usually bestrewed with the choicest flowers that the meadows of Glossop Dale can produce, and liberally furnished with flags and streamers. Thus prepared, it is drawn through the different parts of the village, preceded by groups of dancers and a band of music. All the ribbons in the place may be said to be in requisition on this festive day; and he who is the greatest favourite among the lasses is generally the gayest personage in the cavalcade. After parading the village, the car stops at the church gates, where it is dismantled of its honours. The rushes and flowers are then taken into church, and strewed amongst the pews and along the floors, and the garlands are hung up near the entrance into the chancel in remembrance of the day. The ceremony ended, the various parties who made up the procession retire, amidst music and dancing, to the village inn, where they spend the remainder of the day in joyous festivity."

The garlands remained in church until the next "rush-bearing". One of these garlands was described by Lysons in 1810 as being "chiefly formed of gilt and coloured papers, with glass balls sparkling here and there, and a bird crowning the top."

Some customs seem to have been prompted solely by a spirit of intimidation to obtain personal profit, and appear to have no discernible point or principle by which we may trace or identify their original purpose. Plough Monday activities seem to fall within this category. It used to be the day when Christmas festivities were terminated and the rural population resumed its labours. It was originally observed the day after Plough Sunday, but this date appears to have become flexible and varied in some villages. At Tideswell it was observed on the first Monday after New Year's Day and the custom was known to be carried out in 1881 and as recently as 1901. But at Stoney Middleton it was recognised on the day before Shrove Tuesday, and was also known as "Collop Monday" because on this day farmers were solicited for "collops" of bacon, eggs and milk required for making pancakes the next day.

Teams of young farm labourers known as "plough bullocks" were yoked to a small plough which they dragged around the villages, threatening to plough up the thresholds or doorsteps of houses if the residents refused them money with which to ransom their property from such damage. The young men wore neither coats nor jackets, and their shirts were smothered with multi-coloured rosettes, while their hats were decorated with ribbands and an assortment of other ornaments. The company included a fool who was dressed in a calf-skin and carried an inflated bladder on the end of a whip, and this was used to belabour the heads and shoulders of the team when they showed any pretended recalcitrance. Another character was Bessie, a male masquerading in feminine attire whose antics added to the farce.

"Clay-daubin' " was a custom which marked the weddings of young couples and assured them of having, at least, a roof over their heads. After the marriage ceremony held in the morning, relatives, guests and well-wishers assembled to erect a home for the newly wed. So many people were involved, and such was the degree of enthusiasm and energy of the workers, that the dwelling was erected the same day and made ready for occupation. Upon completion of their task, the assembled company shared in what festive cheer the occasion could afford. From this modest beginning, the cottage grew and was enlarged as financial circumstances improved and the necessity of family life demanded. Further rooms were added, along with an occasional outhouse, so that each cottage acquired its own distinctive character and architectural charm.

11. Christmas Customs and Carols

PEAKLANDERS of the past have always acknowledged the coronation of Christmas as the most important event in the calendar of the Church, even though many of them have favoured feasting rather than fasting, and laid emphasis on the secular rather than the sacred character of the festival. At every level of society it has been recognised as an occasion for music, mirth and merriment; for gaiety, greetings and goodwill. It gave opportunity for the rich man in his castle to remember the poor man at his gate, and provided an oasis of light in the desert of dark and dreary days of winter. As far back as the 17th century, Philip Kinder wrote of Peaklanders: — "They love their cards. The miners at Christmas tyme will carry tenn or twenty pounds about them, game freely, returne home againe, all the year after good husbands." But there have also been those of studious mind and serious disposition who "rejoiced with exceeding great joy" along with the Wise Men, patiently watching with the shepherds by their camp-fires and listening with rapture to the angelic melodies of heaven. And as a result of their meditation upon the eternal mysteries of the Incarnation, they have bequeathed to posterity a wealth of carol literature and music.

About four hundred years ago, a Steward of Haddon Hall left a hint of the Christmas preparations made in his day, when he entered into his accounts: — "Payde ye xxijth daye of December vnto Roger Jackson of assheborne for one qwartor of beyffe to be powdered ... xijs."

Alleyn Sutton composed a ballad which was sung when the boar's head— crest of the Vernons—was served each Christmas. It begins: —

> A grislie bore, as raven's feathers black,
> Bred in that land Rollo had by his wyfe,
> Paste th' ocean sea, the bastard's part to take,
> That Harrolde refte of kingdome and of lyfe ...

The passing centuries saw little change at Haddon. The same atmosphere of festive cheer continued to prevail, and a century after the above records had been filed, another steward added the chronicle of Christmas activities for the year 1663:— "Pd. George Wood the Cook for helping in the pantry all Christmas ... £3. Pd. Robert Swindell for helping at like work all Christmas and two weeks £1 5s. Pd. Wid. Creswick for pulling Fowls and Pulling all Christmas ... 3s. 6d. Pd. Thos Shaw the Piper for pipering all Christmas ... £2. Given by their Honors command to Ottiwel Bromwall the Dancer ... 10s. Given by their Honors command to Ottiwel Bromwall's Kinswoman for Dancing ... 5s."

One of the Earls of Rutland, when presiding at Christmas celebrations, used to sing the couplet:—

You're all heartily welcome, lads, drink what you will;
For here lives John in his wooden nook still.

Those who declined the Rutland hospitality, or those who presumed upon it, were treated with short shrift. Attached to the wainscoting of the banqueting-hall can still be seen the manacle by which those who refused the Earl's beer were handcuffed while the spurned beverage was poured down their sleeves.

One Christmas during the 17th century, a Darley Dale butcher named John Taylor was punished in a salutary manner for repeated thefts of butter from the Hall. Taylor was a corpulent man weighing eighteen stones, and visited Haddon each week to supply the household with meat. At that period, butter was always left in what is now the banqueting-hall awaiting a routine inspection by the Earl's wife before being transferred to the larder. Two butlers had noticed for several weeks that two pounds of butter were regularly missing and decided to keep watch to try and find the culprit. They concealed themselves at different vantage points where it was possible to observe the movements of all who entered the room. Being Christmas, open house was kept so that the room was occupied by many people coming and going. When the butcher made his appearance, he was seen to glance cautiously round the assembled company before choosing a convenient moment to furtively transfer a pound of butter to each of his capacious pockets, and then mingled innocently with the rest of the callers. Knowing that their master would have possibly forgiven the butcher without any confrontation, the butlers decided to administer their own justice, and Taylor was invited into the kitchen and given a seat close to the fire.

"Jack," commented the senior butler, "'tis Christmas time. I have a famous jack of strong beer and you shall taste it e'er you leave. Stay here while I fetch it from the cellar."

After consuming the flagon of beer, the uneasy butcher would

70

gladly have vacated his seat by the blazing fire, but was pressed to take more beer. Soon the melting butter began to seep down his breeches and stockings into his shoes. Remarking that he looked slimmer on one side than the other, the butler insisted upon the poor fellow changing sides, whereupon the other pound was speedily reduced to a stalactitic flow and oozed from the discomfited butcher's shoes as he finally took his departure from the Hall.

At Renishaw Hall, home of the Sitwells, preparations for Christmas began early in November with the brewing of a couple of hogsheads of Christmas beer, and the making of a "brawne"—valued at £2—which was equivalent in price to four muttons and forty turkeys. During the festive season, the Chester-field and Staveley fiddlers were engaged to play for dancing; gifts were made to the servants; money disbursed to the poor of the parish; and turkeys, fowls and rolls of brawn were sent as "tokens" to absent friends.

Turning from the magnificent meals served in the mansions, to the homelier fare of the cottages, we find that Christmas was celebrated on a much less lavish scale, yet with the same spirit of hospitality and goodwill. The season began with the drinking of a posset. This was primarily a Christmas beverage, although its beneficial properties made it a popular drink for winter evenings. It was a protection against chills and helped to induce sleep in those troubled with insomnia. The ingredients of posset included boiled milk or cream, ale, eggs, treacle, ginger, nutmeg and other spices. Posset was drunk on Christmas Eve, and specially designed pots were used for this family communion. Like the loving-cups they had handles on both sides to facilitate passing from one person to another. Sometimes the pots were ornamented with floral designs and often inscribed with the names of the owners and perhaps a couplet such as one originating from Ashford-in-the-Water:

Abraham & Sarah Hollis
Long may we live, happy may we be
Blest with Contentment & from Misfortune free.
Decr. 17, 1819.

Sometimes the pots were made of brown salt glaze ware and were embossed with agricultural scenes.

Robert M. Gilchrist described the making of a posset in one of his short stories:— "Et shall be a posset—a Kirsmus posset i' harvest time. Little else but posset hes been drunk aat o' thee i' my livin' mem'ry. An' et mun be th' strongest posset as thaa'st held i' thy belly for mony a long year. Gin i' et, an' rum, an' whiskey, an' nutmegs, an' cloves, an' ginger. I wunna hev no milk—a gill o' cream wi' lump sugar's th' best. An' a raand o' toast to soften et."

When the Christmas posset was served in homes where there were unattached sons and daughters, a silver coin and ring were placed in the pot, and each person took a spoonful in turn. The recovery of the ring was supposed to augur well for an early and happy marriage, while the one fortunate enough to scoop up the coin was assured of a prosperous future.

One lady told me an amusing—if that is the correct adjective—incident which happened one Christmas morning after her family had partaken of posset the night before. A bowl containing the remains of the posset had been left on the sideboard, and when they came downstairs they were puzzled to find the wall patterned with a frescoe which might have been conceived by some student of surrealist art. The mystery of the strange decor was solved when it was found that rats had been paddling in the posset during the night, and had produced the design with their feet and tails—perhaps during some drunken orgy!

Incidentally, posset was one of the medicines used during Eyam Plague, and a story is told of one patient who, having narrowly escaped premature burial by Marshall Howe, the self-appointed undertaker and sexton, recovered after drinking a posset.

At Bradwell the posset-drinking ceremony was illuminated by the burning of yule-logs and a special Christmas candle supplied by the village grocer to each of his customers. The family also had a yule loaf which consisted of a round loaf on top of a four-pound loaf, both baked together, and sometimes surmounted with a figure. The first two customs no doubt had some significance with the pagan festival of rejoicing at the victory of light over darkness at the turn of the winter solstice.

Christmas Eve was also recognised in some villages as "mischief night" when a certain amount of liberty was claimed for roguery and pranks played by village youths under cover of darkness. Gates were removed from their hinges; doors were securely fastened from the outside; water-butts were overturned; carts dispossessed of their wheels; sods dropped down convenient chimneys, and many other wilful acts were committed. Householders were equally alert, however, and sometimes the mischief makers were caught and chastised by angry victims.

At Tideswell the owner of a cart watched several youths taking his vehicle from the Town Head with the intention of pitching it into a stream in Manchester Road. Just as they were on the point of fulfilling their mission, the practical jokers were dismayed at the sudden appearance of the owner, and not a little discomfited when he insisted upon their restoring the cart to its proper quarters. A former Bradwell farmer was less fortunate. Seeing a party of youths trundling a cart down Smalldale to deposit it in the brook, he decided to join in the fun. Upon reaching the verge of the stream, he suddenly realised that it was his own cart. "Hey, steady on. Stop lads," he remonstrated, "t' cart's mine!" But it was too late and the cart was heaved into the stream.

Christmas was an occasion when distributions were made under the terms of charitable bequests, and the poor received gifts of food or footwear, clothing or coal, or sums of money. Under the conditions of the 17th century will of Thomas Large, the Mayor of Chesterfield was directed to provide a convenient house for three poor persons who each received an annuity of £5 together with the gift of a blue cloth gown at Christmas. In the same town, inmates of the almshouses provided by Sarah Rose were furnished with a Christmas present of new gowns with the initials "S.R." worked on the right sleeves. Occupants of the St. John's Hospital at Bakewell must have been proud as peacocks (crest of their patron) as they walked to church in their new Christmas gowns, each with a yellow and blue cross embroidered on the left breast, and with the instruction that these were to be worn at all times except when the owners were working. And there must have been envious glances cast at the inmates of Wilmot's almshouses at Derby who not only received new black gowns faced with red, but a share in thirty yards of linen cloth for the making of shirts and smocks, and, to keep them warm within, a Christmas dinner. Furthermore, for good measure, they were the recipients of a new red cap each alternate year. Then at Melbourne, Henry Greene directed that four green waistcoats lined with green galloon lace should be given to four poor women on or before the 21st December. Thomas Gray went a step further, for he provided six waistcoats of grey cloth to be faced with baize or "some other blue stuff" for the poor widows of Castle Donington and Melbourne.

"Guising" or "mumming", as the custom is alternatively called, reminds us again of a semi-pagan ritual performed at the turn of the winter solstice to celebrate the victory of light over darkness. In different parts of Derbyshire the characters of the play varied, and followed such themes as the Derby Ram or the Story of St. George and the Dragon. Some authorities think that the custom is a survival of an ancient miracle or mystery play. Groups of performers, suitably disguised, used to visit village homes to present their play. The St. George version included such characters as Slasher the Soldier, the Black Prince of Paladine, and Hector, who were three adversaries of the patron saint. A Doctor and Fool played their part, as well as Little Devil Dout who was dressed in black and brandished a besom or three-grained fork. Needless to say, such plays were subject to much adaptation and

73

no little improvisation if the group exceeded the recognised number of players. The introductory lines usually ran:

> Room, room, brave gallants, give us room to sport,
> For in this room we wish to resort,
> Resort and repeat to you our merry rhyme,
> For remember, good Sirs, this is Christmas time;
> The time to cut goose pies doth now appear,
> So we are come to act our Merry Christmas here.
> At the sound of the trumpet, and beat of the drum.
> Make room, brave gentlemen, and let our actors come.
> We are merry actors that show pleasant play,
> Step in St. George, and show the way.

St. George then made his entry with the announcement:

> I am St. George, who from old England sprung,
> My famous name throughout the world hath rung:
> Many bloody deeds and wonders have I made known
> And made tyrants tremble on their throne.

After an affray with Slasher the Soldier, St. George proves victorious and the services of a physician are requested. For a stated fee, the Doctor claims that he is able to "cure the Itch, the Stitch, the Palsy and the Gout, and if a man has 19 devils in his skull, he guarantees to cast 20 of them out ..."

The next combatant was the Black Prince who introduced himself:

> I am the Black Prince of Paladine, born of high renown,
> Soon I will fetch St. George's lofty courage down.
> Before St. George shall be received by me—
> St. George shall die to all eternity.

But this challenger is also duly despatched, as is Hector, following which Little Devil Dout appears with either besom or fork, uttering the threat:

> Here comes I, little Devil Dout,
> If you don't give me money, I'll sweep you all out:
> Money I want, and money I crave—
> If you don't give me money, I'll sweep you to the grave.

There is a great variety of versions of the Derby Ram, or Derby Tup, but they all follow the same basic pattern. The dialogue included both mime and music, and was sometimes introduced by the Leader announcing:

> *Here comes me an' ahr owd lass,*
> *Short o' money an' short o' brass:*
> *Gather around us and come close up*
> *And we will perform you the Derby Tup.*

Then the performers sang the ballad which had a varying number of verses and began:

> *As I was going to market upon a market day,*
> *I met the finest ram, Sir, that ever was fed on hay ...*

The characters included a blacksmith with hammer and tongs; a butcher with knife and apron; and another performer covered with a curtain or sack through which protruded a broom stale upon which was impaled a ram's head, or one carved from wood and having glass eyes. The highlight of the performance was the slaying of the ram; an incident thought by some antiquaries to date from the days when a ram was cut up and divided among the poor, or from earlier days of ritualistic animal sacrifices. Some writers have suggested that the play may have some astrological significance in relation to the constellation of Aries. The people of Derby used to gild the horns of their rams when performing the play, giving rise to the conjecture that this may have been a survival of the Roman custom of gilding the horns of sacrificial animals.

In the south of the county, the St. George mummers introduced themselves with a somewhat different verse, but evidently from some ancestral script:

> *I open the door, I enter in,*
> *I trust your favour I shall win.*
> *Whether I sit, stand, rise or fall,*
> *I'll do my duty to please you all.*
> *A room, a room, a gallant room; a room to let us in;*
> *Stir up the fire and make a light*
> *And see our noble act tonight.*
> *If you can't believe the words I say,*
> *Step in King George—and clear the way.*

We notice that in this version the saint has become king, while a newcomer to the scene is a young Turk and the Black Prince is replaced by the Princess of Paradise. There is the familiar doctor who states his qualifications as:

My name is Doctor M. D. Brown,
The finest doctor in the town.
I cure the hip, the grip, the grunts, the gout.
I'll turn your belly inside out.

The play concludes with an announcement by Old Belzebub and is followed by a collection. This character is a variation of Little Devil Dout.

In comes old Belzebub. On my shoulder I carry a club.
In my hand a dripping-pan, and I think myself a jolly old man.
Hink, tink, tink and a sup more to drink.
And I'll make this pan cry "sock".
Apples and nuts, apples and nuts,
When a man's married he stuffs his guts.
Blankets and pins: blankets and pins,
When a man's married his sorrow begins.
My mother has gone washing, my father's at home,
So give us some money and we will all be gone.

There is something of infinite charm in the muted music of either vocal or instrumental melodies heard in the stillness of a frosty, star-lit night. It has a timeless quality which makes every star a shining herald of mysterious magi travelling with gold and spices from distant countries; converting each lamp-lit stable into a place where the miracle of the Incarnation might just have happened, and filling the air with such a sense of awe and expectancy that it would be hardly surprising to meet a group of shepherds discussing in hushed tones a vision of angels.

Carol-making was a more cultural contribution to Christmas than the merry-making of the mummers. It had a dignity and charm that was altogether lacking in their masquerade as they petitioned for alms with blackened faces, comic costume, boisterous antics and doggerel dialogue. It broke away from the relics of the pagan Yuletide, and led men's thoughts in a spiritual pilgrimage to the birthplace of the royal Babe of Bethlehem, reminding them that the season was an occasion of religious rejoicing for a greater victory of light over darkness than that recognised in the revels of pagan worship. This is reinforced by a verse of an 18th century carol from Castleton contained in the *Oxford Book of Carols*:

> *All you that are to mirth inclined,*
> *Consider well and bear in mind*
> *What our good God for us hath done,*
> *In sending His beloved Son.*

During past years we find that Christmas has inspired Peakland poets and minstrels to produce an ever increasing accumulation of literature and music enshrined in local carols, and, although the modern critic may be inclined to despise these homespun compositions, they help to mirror the degree of culture achieved by ordinary people under difficult conditions. They represent a facet of folklore which reflects a period when education was beginning to give coherency to a hitherto unprivileged section of the community. For many Peakland carols were produced when Penny Readings, Methodist class-meetings, and Mechanics' Institutes were the chief source of education for the adult population. A carpenter, a currier, a draper, a grocer and a shoemaker were among those who made contributions to the anthology of carols which, so far, have survived extinction. For it is surprising how that, within a relatively short time, the authorship of some carols has become confused and in some cases totally obscured by circumstantial anonymity. Music and words have been remembered, but the names of the carol-makers forgotten.

There are some instances where the music only is local in character, as, for example, a tune composed by Mr. George Dawson, of Eyam, to the words of "Hark, the herald angels sing". This melody suddenly invaded the composer's mind while engaged at his occupation of shoe-making. Snatching up a leather sole in the absence of more conventional writing material, he jotted down the cascade of notes on this very unusual manuscript material.

Many of the carols have been sung for years without careful reference to their musical settings, and examination of the original scores shows how the music has often been changed in character and quality over a period of years until there are quite distinct differences in interpretation. This also applies— perhaps in a lesser degree—to the words. In some instances the sense of certain phrases has been completely altered by the omission of some words and the introduction of others due to careless and slipshod repetition.

One might imagine that the introduction of various modern hymnals would have helped to standardise Christmas hymns by providing a uniform selection of words and music. But Derbyshire has always been proud of its anthologies of Christmas carols, and each village has been jealous to preserve its own collection. I have in my possession a manuscript carol book which has tattered covers and dog-eared corners. Its pages are stained; the ink of its "hand-pricked" notes is faded and brown; the copper-plate verses are blurred and stained by exposure to the weather, and there are frequent errors in spelling. The book once belonged to the fiddler who accompanied the carollers round our village at Christmas.

William Newton, the Abney-born "Minstrel of the Peak", and Richard Furness, a native of Eyam, each celebrated Christmas by writing a carol. Furness wrote the words and music of more than thirty carols, while Samuel Slack, the renowned bass singer of Tideswell, supplied the music for several of Newton's productions. Here is a verse of one of them:

Hymn for Christmas Day, 1797

On the radiant wings of Morn
Love and Grace divine are born,
The spheres celestial ring,
Golden Harps from all the sky
Speak the great Messiah nigh,
And Heavenly voices sing,
"From Man to Man let love increase,
To God be Glory, and on Earth be Peace."

At Foolow, the programme of the carol-singers—who begin their tour of the scattered farms and cottages at midnight on Christmas Eve—includes a carol written by Richard Furness, which contains the verses:

Joy to the world! The long expected star
Leads on a glorious train from heaven afar,
'Tis Jacob's star that cheers the gloomy night,
And sheds o'er all mankind its living light.

Wake all ye choirs, your vocal incense bring
And strike the golden lyre with dulcet string;
Lift up your heads ye abject and forlorn,
A Saviour, Prophet, Priest and King is born.

In the neighbouring village of Eyam where Furness was born, the above carol is quite unfamiliar to the carol parties, yet they sing one of his compositions entitled "Hail, delightful sacred morn" which is equally unknown in Foolow, and at the next village of Stoney Middleton, an established favourite was a Furness carol beginning "Awake my Harp, my Voice and cheerful Lute" which was totally strange to the two previous villages.

As time went on, some of the carol-makers escaped from the conventional theme of angels and shepherds and wise men. They began to forsake the stable and the star, leaving the pastoral scenes of Palestine and venturing into the warmth and comfort of contemporary Peakland homes to capture the sights, sounds and scents of Christmas. Mr. J. T. Hancock, an Eyam draper, wrote the lilting words of the following carol, and also the music which has an equally lively quality. It not only helps to illustrate the changing idiom, but is an example of the way in which local carols are slipping through our fingers, for, although it has been sung in comparatively recent years, none of the singers can recall the first verse:

> *Merry, merry Christmas everywhere!*
> *Cheerily it ringeth through the air;*
> > *Christmas bells, Christmas trees,*
> > *Christmas odours on the breeze.*
> *Why should we, so joyfully, sing with grateful mirth?*
> *See, the Sun of Righteousness beams upon the earth.*

Here is another carol which, quite unwittingly no doubt, does not even hint at the sacred story which is the centre and soul of Christmas. It is purely secular in character, yet charmingly illustrates the mood of the season:

> *A song, a joyous song to thee,*
> > *Old Christmas now we sing,*
> *With minstrel rhymes and merry chimes,*
> > *We herald thee a king.*
> *A crown of laurel decks thy brow,*
> > *As green as sunny woods;*
> *And mistletoe with pearls aglow,*
> > *'Mid coral holly buds.*

> ### CHORUS
> > *Then once again a song to thee*
> > *Old Christmas now we sing,*
> > *With minstrel rhymes and merry chimes,*
> > *We herald thee a king.*

> *Old Christmas dear, there's greeting here,*
> > *From wealthy and from poor,*
> *From royal domes and cottage homes,*
> > *A pledge of fealty sure.*
> *From minster chanting rich and full,*
> > *From simple village choir;*
> *From royal band in palace grand,*
> > *Or group by cottage fire.*

Unfortunately many carol-makers have hung their harps on the willow trees. Traditional carols were once regarded as family heirlooms; treasured by one generation, but perhaps discarded by the next. Popular with parents, but scorned by children. And because there have been few chroniclers of Christmas carols, and

79

few archives of village history where they might be safely preserved, the number has steadily been reduced by the combined attacks of damp, dust, decay and indifference. And we are forced to the conclusion that the art of making carols, like the crafts of thatching and mear-making, belongs to a generation that is dead and gone. But, instead of lamenting the passing of this rustic art, let us hope for its re-birth and a revival of the enthusiasm which produced such words as these: —

> *We twine our festive garlands*
> *For the happy Christmas morn,*
> *When bloom'd the Rose of Sharon*
> *And the Holy One was born;*
> *When tidings of Salvation*
> *Burst the Captive's prison bands,*
> *When valleys were exalted*
> *And the mountains clapp'd their hands.*

CHORUS

> *Saints in robes of white are singing*
> *Hear their loud hosannas ring;*
> *Earth her richest store is bringing*
> *To the temple of her king.*

> *His birth was meek and lowly*
> *And a manger was His bed;*
> *The Son of Man, our Saviour*
> *Had not where to lay His head:*
> *He came to seek and save us,*
> *He will take our sins away,*
> *He came the sheep to gather*
> *Who had wandered far away.*

> *All glory in the highest*
> *Was the burden of their song;*
> *On Judah's plain that echoed*
> *From the shining angel throng:*
> *Oh, let our hearts be joyful*
> *While we swell the note again—*
> *All glory in the highest*
> *And on earth goodwill to men.*